Light Manufacturing in Zambia

DIRECTIONS IN DEVELOPMENT
Private Sector Development

Light Manufacturing in Zambia

Job Creation and Prosperity in a Resource-Based Economy

Hinh T. Dinh
with contributions by Praveen Kumar, Anna Morris, Fahrettin Yagci, and
Kathleen Fitzgerald

THE WORLD BANK
Washington, D.C.

Contents

Figures

Tables

Foreword

This book on light manufacturing in Zambia is part of broader World Bank work on light manufacturing in Africa. The focus on light manufacturing, with its emphasis on labor-intensive economic activities, is particularly appropriate for a resource-based economy such as that of Zambia. While Zambia's recent growth has been impressive, it has not been accompanied with adequate job creation. The long-term job creation in copper production has been small; links to the rest of the economy tend to be weak as well; and the development of natural resources tends to discourage job-creating sectors such as manufacturing in any case. This book argues that, to be sustainable and to create productive employment, growth needs to be accompanied by structural transformation. Such transformation entails a growing share of manufacturing output in the economy.

In the past, Zambia's efforts to promote and facilitate industrial growth were not successful. Policy regimes swung from one extreme to another. In the 1980s, the industrial sector was put under the complete control of the state. When this model proved unsuccessful, the policy shifted in the opposite direction in the 1990s, and all earlier government interventions were lifted. Neither extreme led to sustained growth in manufacturing. This book suggests an alternative: directing government policies toward removing constraints in a few of the most promising light manufacturing sectors using practical, cutting-edge solutions. These solutions would be inspired in part by the experience of the rapidly growing Asian economies that started out at a point 20 years ago not so different from Zambia's level of development in these areas today.

This book has several innovative features. First, it provides in-depth cost comparisons between Zambia and four other countries in Africa and Asia at the sector and product levels. Second, the book uses a wide array of quantitative and qualitative techniques to identify key constraints to enterprises and to evaluate differences in the performance of firms across countries. Third, it uses a focused approach to identify country- and industry-specific constraints. It proposes market-based measures and selected government interventions to ease these constraints. Fourth, it highlights the interconnectedness of constraints and solutions. For example, solving the manufacturing input problem requires actions in agriculture, education, and infrastructure.

The book shows that Zambia has the potential to become regionally competitive in several light manufacturing subsectors by leveraging its comparative advantage in natural resource industries such as agriculture, livestock, and forestry. Relevant interventions include both the provision of public goods and the removal of existing policy distortions in the economy. Growing the production of light manufacturing goods would allow Zambia to capture more value from its raw materials and create more jobs.

Kundhavi Kadiresan
Country Director for Zambia, Malawi, and Zimbabwe
Africa Region, The World Bank

Acknowledgments

This book is a part of the Project on Light Manufacturing in Africa conducted by a core team consisting of Hinh T. Dinh (Lead Economist and Team Leader), Vincent Palmade (Lead Economist and Co-Team Leader), Vandana Chandra (Senior Economist), Frances Cossar (Junior Professional), Tugba Gurcanlar (Finance Specialist), Ali Zafar (Senior Economist), Eleonora Mavroeidi (Junior Professional), and Gabriela Calderon Motta (Program Assistant). The Zambia team includes, in addition to the above staff, Praveen Kumar, Anna Morris, Fahrettin Yagci, and Kathleen Fitzgerald. The work was carried out with the support and guidance of the following senior managers of the World Bank: Justin Yifu Lin (former Senior Vice President and Chief Economist), Oby Ezekwesili (former Vice President, Africa Region), Kaushik Basu (Senior Vice President and Chief Economist), Makhtar Diop (Vice President, Africa Region), Kundhavi Kadiresan (Country Director, Zambia, Malawi, and Zimbabwe), Shanta Devarajan (Chief Economist, Africa Region), Zia Qureshi (Director, Operations and Strategy, Development Economics), Gaiv Tata (Director, Africa Finance and Private Sector Development), and Marilou Uy (Senior Advisor, Special Envoy Office and Former Director, Africa Finance and Private Sector Development). The report findings are based on a number of missions to Lusaka. The July 2009 mission included Vandana Chandra, Hinh T. Dinh (Team Leader), Alan Gelb, Tugba Gurcanlar, Vincent Palmade (Co-Team Leader), Gaël Raballand, and Marilou Uy. Subsequent missions were led by Hinh T. Dinh and Fahrettin Yagci. Detailed cross-country value chain analyses were provided by Global Development Solutions, LLC of Reston, Virginia under the direction of Yasuo Konishi, Glen Surabian, and David Phillips. We thank participants at the Light Manufacturing in Zambia Workshop held in Lusaka in December 2012 for their valuable comments. We thank the following Bank staff for their unfailing support: Alphonsus J. Marcelis, Célestin Monga, David Rosenblatt, Geremie Sawadogo, Dipankar Megh Bhanot, Aban Daruwala, Saida Doumbia Gall, Nancy Lim, and Melanie Brah Marie Melindji.

The report benefited from key inputs by Hon. Robert Sichinga (Minister of Commerce, Trade, and Industry), Stephen Mwansa (Permanent Secretary, Ministry of Commerce, Trade, and Industry), Roseta Mwape (Chief Executive Officer, Zambia Association of Manufacturers), Brian Mtonya (Senior Private Sector Development Specialist, East and Southern Africa), Asumani Guloba

(Economist, Africa Finance and Private Sector Development), John Sutton (London School of Economics), Marie Sheppard, Scott Rockafellow, the Global Development Solutions team (Washington, DC), and the following in Zambia: Robert Banda (Director, Zambia Development Agency), Caiaphas Habasonda (Chief Investment Officer, Development Bank of Zambia), Andrew Levin (Economic Growth Team Leader, United States Agency for International Development) Aloys Lorkeers (First Counselor, European Union), Ville Luukkanen (Counselor, Embassy of Finland), Chilambwe Lwao (Program Officer, European Union), Windu Matuka (Director, Zambia Development Agency), Glyne Michelo (Director, Zambia Development Agency), John Mulongoti (Director, Ministry of Commerce, Trade, and Industry), Florance Mumba (Director, Zambia Development Agency), Noah Mutoti (Deputy Director, Bank of Zambia), Roseta Mwape (Chief Executive Officer, Zambia Association of Manufacturers), Muyanmbango Nkwema (Chief Economist, Ministry of Commerce, Trade, and Industry), Goodson Sinyenga (Deputy Director, Central Statistical Office), and Mchokoliso Tembo (Treasurer, Economics Association of Zambia).

The report was edited by a team headed by Robert Zimmermann and Meta deCoquereaumont. The financial support of the Bank-Netherlands Partnership Program and the Japan Policy and Human Resources Development Fund is gratefully acknowledged.

About the Author and Contributors

About the Author

Hinh T. Dinh is Lead Economist in the Office of the Senior Vice President and Chief Economist of the World Bank. Previously, he served as Lead Economist in the Africa Region (1998–2008), the Finance Complex (1991–98), and the Middle East and North Africa Region at the World Bank (1979–81). He received his undergraduate degrees with high honors in economics and mathematics from the State University of New York and his M.A. in economics, M.S. in industrial engineering, and PhD in economics from the University of Pittsburgh. His research focuses on public finance, international finance, industrialization, and economic development. His latest books include *Light Manufacturing in Africa* (2012), *Performance of Manufacturing Firms in Africa* (2012), and *Tales from the Development Frontier* (2013).

About the Contributors

Praveen Kumar is Lead Economist for Zambia in the World Bank Country Office in Lusaka, Zambia. He previously served as Lead Economist for Kenya and Zimbabwe. He holds a PhD in economics from the University of Maryland, College Park.

Anna Morris is currently a Senior Advisor on energy policy to the New Zealand government. Between 2009 and 2011, she was a consultant at the World Bank, including two years based in the World Bank's Zambia Country Office. Previously, she worked as an advisor to the government of Guyana under the Overseas Development Institute's Fellowship Scheme, as an economic consultant at the Brattle Group, and at Her Majesty's Treasury in London. She has an MSc from the London School of Economics and an M.A. from Oxford University.

Fahrettin Yagci is a World Bank retiree currently teaching economics at Bosphorus University, Istanbul. He worked on 20 countries in Africa, Asia, Europe, and the Middle East during his 22 years of service at the World Bank. His areas of responsibility included trade policy, industrial policy, agriculture, and macroeconomics. Before joining the World Bank, he taught economics at several universities in Ankara and Istanbul and also worked for the Turkish government. He received his PhD in economics from the London School of Economics.

Kathleen Fitzgerald is a research consultant at the World Bank. She received her undergraduate degree in economics and international relations at Simmons College and her MSc in development economics at the School of Oriental and African Studies, University of London. Her research interests include economic development, international health, and women's studies in the African and South Asian regions of the World Bank.

Abbreviations

CEEC	Citizens Economic Empowerment Commission (Zambia)
DBZ	Development Bank of Zambia
DRC	domestic resource cost
GDP	gross domestic product
RCA	revealed comparative advantage
SNDP	Sixth National Development Plan (Zambia)
ZAFFICO	Zambia Forestry and Forest Industries Corporation
ZDA	Zambia Development Agency

Note: All dollar amounts are U.S. dollars ($) unless otherwise indicated.

CHAPTER 1

The Potential of Light Manufacturing in Africa

Introduction

This report on Zambia is part of a broader World Bank project on light manufacturing in Africa (Dinh and others 2012).[1]

After stagnating for most of the past 45 years, economic performance in Sub-Saharan Africa is at a turning point. The reforms of the 1990s across much of Sub-Saharan Africa that focused on macroeconomic stability and liberalization gained traction during the first decade of the 2000s. From 2001 to 2010, the region's gross domestic product (GDP) grew at an average rate of 5.2 percent a year, and per capita income increased 2 percent a year (up from an average of −0.4 percent in the 1990s). Net foreign direct investment totaled $33 billion, almost five times the $7 billion over 1990–99, and export growth was robust.[2]

Experience shows that such growth cannot be sustained without a structural transformation that lifts workers from low-productivity jobs in the informal sector to higher-productivity activities. This transformation has yet to take place in Sub-Saharan Africa. The boom in the commodities that are Sub-Saharan Africa's primary exports (such as oil, cotton, metals, and minerals) fueled a large part of the growth in the last decade. Investment remains low, less than 15 percent of GDP, compared with 25 percent in Asia, and more than 80 percent of workers are stranded in low-productivity jobs.

Labor-intensive light manufacturing led the economic transformation of most high-performing developing countries; yet, it has not fared well in Sub-Saharan Africa. While China's dominance of global manufacturing in recent years has shrunk the market share of other regions, the contraction in Sub-Saharan Africa's share has been longer and deeper than most. Sub-Saharan Africa's share of global light manufacturing has dwindled to less than 1 percent, and preferential access to markets in the European Union and the United States has made little difference. Without structural transformation, Sub-Saharan Africa is unlikely to catch up with more prosperous countries, such as China and Vietnam, which were not so different economically in the 1980s relative to Sub-Saharan Africa today.

In addition to increasing the productivity of medium and large formal firms, Sub-Saharan Africa has to raise the productivity and encourage the upgrading and expansion of micro and small enterprises, most of them in the informal sector. Light manufacturing in Sub-Saharan Africa is characterized by a few formal medium firms providing products for niche or protected markets and a vast number of small informal, low-productivity firms providing low-quality products for domestic markets. These small enterprises provide low-paying jobs, little in foreign exchange earnings, and few productive employment opportunities. Encouragement for the productivity and expansion of small firms has not received adequate attention. It is addressed in this report.

This study draws on the following five analytical tools[3]:

- The World Bank Enterprise Surveys[4]
- Qualitative interviews with about 300 enterprises (both formal and informal) of all sizes in China, Ethiopia, Tanzania, Vietnam, and Zambia, conducted by the study team and based on a questionnaire designed by John Sutton of the London School of Economics
- Quantitative interviews with about 1,400 enterprises (formal and informal) of all sizes in the same five countries, conducted by the Centre for the Study of African Economies at Oxford University and based on a questionnaire designed by Marcel Fafchamps and Simon Quinn of Oxford University
- In-depth interviews with about 300 formal medium enterprises in the same five countries that focused on the value chain and that were conducted by Global Development Solutions
- A study of the impact of Kaizen managerial training among owners of small and medium enterprises; this training, delivered to about 250 entrepreneurs in Ethiopia, Tanzania, and Vietnam, was led by Japanese researchers from the Foundation for Advanced Studies on International Development and the National Graduate Institute for Policy Studies

Five features distinguish our study from previous studies. First, the detailed examination of light manufacturing at the sector and product levels in five countries provides in-depth cost comparisons between Africa and Asia. Second, building on a growing body of work, the study uses a wide array of quantitative and qualitative techniques, including surveys and value chain analysis, to identify key constraints to enterprises and to evaluate differences in firm performance across countries. Third, the finding that firm constraints vary by country, sector, and firm size leads to a focused approach to the identification of constraints and the adoption of a combination of market-based measures and government interventions to remove them. Fourth, the study recognizes that improving the prospects for light manufacturing requires actions across many sectors, not only manufacturing. Solving the problems of manufacturing inputs means solving specific issues in agriculture, education, and infrastructure. Fifth, the study draws on experiences and solutions in other developing countries to inform its recommendations. The goal is to find practical ways to increase employment and spur job creation in Sub-Saharan Africa.

At a broad level, in the three African countries covered—Ethiopia, Tanzania, and Zambia—and across sectors and firms of varying sizes, the study identifies six binding constraints to the growth of light manufacturing: input availability, cost, and quality; access to industrial land; access to finance; trade logistics; entrepreneurial skills; and worker skills. The combinations of these six constraints vary by country, sector, and firm size. For example, entrepreneurial skills, land, inputs, and finance are the most important constraints among small firms, while trade logistics, land, and inputs are among the most important among large firms.

This finding has two implications. First, policy makers need to identify the constraints in specific sectors to design effective policies to remove them. Second, once these constraints have been identified, it becomes clear that they are few in number, are fairly easily addressed, and can create a chain reaction of reforms. This contrasts with past studies of Africa's growth potential, which have resulted in a long list of constraints, including infrastructure, education, corruption, and red tape. Our findings point to a smaller number of more specific constraints and, sometimes, new key constraints. Narrowing the analysis can make the reform agenda more manageable given the financial and human resource limitations of most African countries.

The report presents an in-depth diagnosis of the constraints in five light manufacturing sectors in Zambia: apparel, leather products, wood products, metal products, and agribusiness. These sectors have been selected because they have the greatest potential; limited resources can be directed at easing the most severe constraints to unleash the energy in these sectors. Policy reforms are proposed based on their success in addressing these constraints in other countries.

In four of the five sectors, the advantage of African countries in lower money wages is wiped out by higher input and trade logistics costs (figure 1.1). The exception, leather products, has the highest share of labor within production costs (45 percent in China, compared with about 20 percent in the other sectors). Among up-to-scale and fairly well-managed companies, the production cost penalty deriving from lower labor productivity is small (except in wood products) because firms are shielded from international competition by high transport costs.

Identifying the binding constraints is the first step in overcoming them. Focusing on removing the constraints in a specific sector or set of sectors trims the long list of challenges to a shorter list that may be dealt with relatively quickly, without creating complex political economy problems in the short run. And this means that Zambia does not need to wait for all issues across all sectors to be dealt with before it embarks on structural transformation.

Because the binding constraints vary by country, sector, and firm size, policy makers need to accomplish the following:

- Identify the most promising manufacturing sectors and then identify, prioritize, and remove the most serious constraints.
- Keep targeted policies selective, consistent with the country's comparative advantage and in line with the country's resources and capacity; use conventional and unconventional policies, such as plug-and-play industrial zones.

Figure 1.1 Sources of Relative Excess Production Costs, Ethiopia, Tanzania, and Zambia, 2011

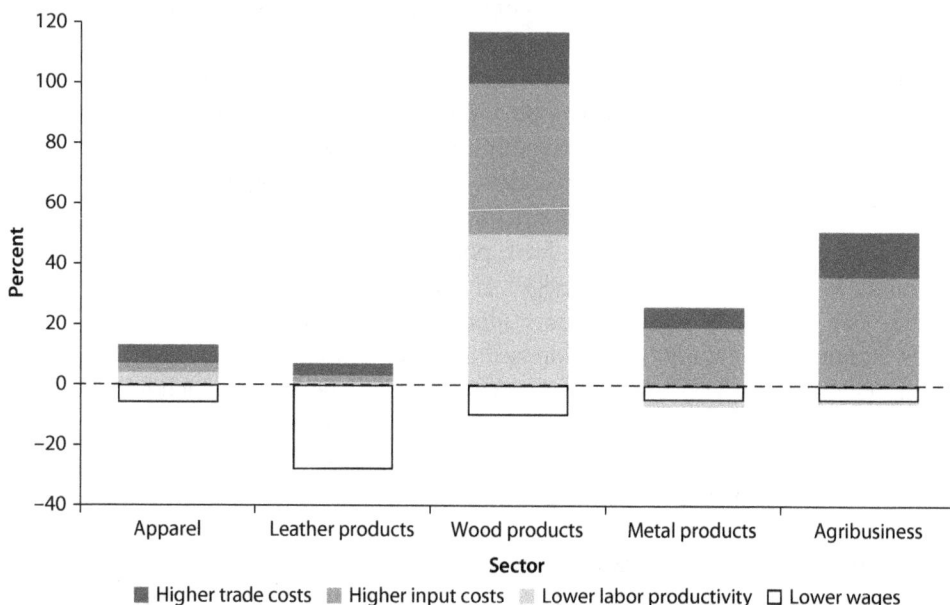

Source: Dinh and others 2012.
Note: The figure shows the average production costs at medium firms in Ethiopia, Tanzania, and Zambia as a percentage of production costs at similar firms in China.

- Start small and build gradually; success breeds success, as the Ethiopian rose farm case study illustrates (see Dinh and others 2012). One person started a rose farm, and now 75 farms produce $200 million in exports and have created 50,000 jobs.

Why Light Manufacturing?[5]

Light manufacturing (including agribusiness) has been an important stepping stone toward economic transformation in most economically successful developing countries (for example, China, Mauritius, Vietnam, and the Asian tigers).[6] Light manufacturing is labor intensive and allows low-income countries to compete by leveraging their low labor costs. As they grow, light manufacturing firms earn and save foreign exchange, provide higher wages to the vast pools of underemployed labor, and develop new technical and managerial skills. In addition to their low labor costs, African countries also have the opportunity to leverage competitive (or potentially competitive) input industries (for example, agricultural products, leather, and wood) to develop competitive light manufacturing industries. In Ethiopia, for example, where the combined export share of coffee and sesame seeds fell from 75 to 25 percent over 1995–2008, this would imply not only diversification from coffee and sesame seeds toward more-processed agricultural and light manufactured products, but also the transformation of exports of live animals and unprocessed hides and skins into leather, a key input for exports of final products such as leather footwear, handbags, belts, and gloves.[7]

Manufacturing has long been recognized as an engine of growth in industrial countries. Nicholas Kaldor's first law of economic growth states that "the faster the rate of growth of the manufacturing sector, the faster will be the rate of growth of . . . [GDP] . . . for fundamental economic reasons connected with induced productivity growth inside and outside the manufacturing sector" (Thirlwall 1983, 345). In a study on economic growth in developed countries, Kuznets (1959) noted that modern economic development is characterized by long periods of rapid output growth that coincide with a structural shift in the composition of output away from agriculture and into manufacturing.

Even in developed countries where the share of manufacturing in output and employment has been stagnant or declining, there is evidence that manufacturing involves more production links with other sectors and the transfer of more production skills than is the case in nonmanufacturing sectors. A U.S. Department of Commerce (1995) study of the effects of changes in final demand on flows of goods and services between and within industries compared between-industry transfers in the production process of manufacturing and nonmanufacturing industries. Using the ratio of gross output required to satisfy a given unit of final demand as a rough indicator of between-industry transfers, the study found that manufacturing had a much higher activity ratio than did nonmanufacturing; manufacturing industries drew more heavily on nonmanufacturing industries than the reverse; and gross output per unit of final demand was higher in manufacturing industries than in nonmanufacturing industries.

Manufacturing may not be the only driver of economic development in every case. Thus, for example, mining (Botswana), information and communication technology (India), and tourism (Cape Verde) have also been important, and copper is a natural resource that Zambia needs to exploit. However, exploiting natural resources rarely creates many jobs. This chapter argues that, even in resource-based countries, there is a clear case for the development of light manufacturing (including agribusiness). In cooperation with the private sector, governments can identify the light manufacturing sectors in which the country could and should compete on the basis of a clear comparative advantage. The private sector should lead the product-level identification, with government in a supporting role.

Light Manufacturing in Africa and in Zambia

Based on World Bank Enterprise Survey data on 89 countries, the manufacturing sector can be classified into low-technology industries (food and beverages, leather, wood processing and wood products, simple metal products, textiles, and garments) and high-technology industries (metal and machinery, electronics, chemical and pharmaceutical products, nonmetal and plastic products, automobiles, parts, and "other manufacturing"). This classification shows that Africa's natural comparative advantage is more likely to be in low-technology than in high-technology manufacturing (Harrison, Lin, and Xu 2012). And light manufacturing has considerably greater employment potential than heavy manufacturing or more sophisticated services.

In most medium-size African countries, light manufacturing can capitalize on human and natural resources to create a large number of more well-paying jobs fairly rapidly for the vast and growing pool of low-skilled workers, many of whom are already employed in low-productivity jobs in the informal sector. The increasing technological complexity of many manufacturing industries since the emergence of the East Asian tiger economies has led some observers to conclude that the case has weakened for light manufacturing as a better source of job creation than agriculture.

But industries such as apparel, footwear, and furniture remain unskilled-labor intensive. These industries continue to employ vast numbers of unskilled workers around the world, even in China (Panagariya 2008).[8] This is evident from the experiences of East Asian and some South Asian countries, where millions of low-skilled, informal workers were lifted out of poverty with the emergence of light manufacturing. For example, in the Chinese provinces of Guangdong and Fujian, the industrial labor force increased from 6 million in 1985 to 11 million at the end of 2001 (likely to be an understatement, given the large number of migrant workers; see Naughton 2007). Official data indicate that 83 million Chinese were employed in the manufacturing sector in 2002 (NBS 2003). Therefore, it makes good sense for governments to collaborate with the private sector to explore the employment potential of light manufacturing.

The strong connection between light manufacturing and trade is another reason for this choice. The case for export-led growth is well established for developing countries (Chenery 1980; Commission on Growth and Development 2008; Harrison and Rodríguez-Clare 2010). In particular, Harrison and Rodríguez-Clare (2010) suggest that more export-oriented countries have grown more rapidly, although establishing causality is difficult. Developing countries also need to import the skills and technology necessary to move up value chains. Finally, there are important learning effects of exposure to global competition.

The focus on simple, labor-intensive light manufacturing is particularly appropriate for a resource-based country such as Zambia because the development of natural resources tends to discourage development in job-creating sectors such as agriculture and manufacturing. Zambia is blessed with an abundance of copper and other mineral resources that can readily generate foreign exchange and government revenue. However, there are many well-known problems associated with managing mineral resources. First, developing natural resources does not generate many jobs, especially the productive jobs needed in economies where unemployment or severe underemployment is high. Second, pressures on the real exchange rate (the Dutch Disease) tend to discourage labor-intensive growth (see below). Third, mineral revenues are volatile and uncertain because of their dependence on international commodity prices. Finally, mineral resources tend to stimulate rent seeking, which, coupled with weak institutions, makes addressing governance issues difficult in developing countries.

The Dutch Disease refers to the change in a country's production structure arising from a large increase in capital inflows or foreign reserves, typically from a natural resource boom, leading to contraction in the tradable sector, usually manufacturing (Corden 1984; Corden and Neary 1982). The increase in natural resource revenues boosts national income and demand, inducing a shift in production from the tradable sector to the nontradable sector and appreciation in the real exchange rate as a result of the higher prices of nontraded goods relative to traded goods. This raises the costs of inputs for the rest of the economy, particularly for the exporting sectors. Because the mineral sector uses fewer inputs and its dependence on domestically produced goods is low, sectors such as manufacturing and agriculture lose their profitability and competitiveness against imports. Ultimately, the nonmineral export sector contracts, the public sector expands, and inflation rises. The adverse impact of resource wealth on tradable sectors is commonly associated with low economic growth.

One feature of some countries affected by the Dutch Disease is the coexistence of high wages in the formal sector and high levels of unemployment or underemployment in the economy. As pointed out by Seers (1964), wages in these countries first rise in the resource sector and then spread to other sectors, making the creation of employment difficult, whether in the public or the private sector. Under normal circumstances, a real devaluation would rectify the situation, but this is usually not feasible in these countries given that the balance of payments is in a favorable position because of mineral exports.

The shift from the manufacturing sector can be detrimental to growth. If resources are depleted or commodity prices fall, competitive manufacturing industries may not be able to spring back as quickly as needed. Technology grows much more slowly in the mineral sector and the nontradable sector than in the nonmineral tradable sector, preventing firms from investing in the tradable sector.

To escape the Dutch Disease, Zambia has to begin a structural shift in production from mining and subsistence farming to modern agriculture, tourism, and, especially, light manufacturing.

Identifying Opportunities in Light Manufacturing

There are a number of ways for policy makers to identify opportunities in light manufacturing to provide support to the private sector. This section describes some common approaches.

For existing products, the concepts of revealed comparative advantage (RCA) and the domestic resource cost (DRC) may be useful for identifying industries where increased production can accelerate industrialization.[9]

The RCA is an index of a country's relative advantage in exporting a commodity. The index, named after Balassa (1965), is defined as follows:

$$RCA = (E_{ij}/E_{iw}) \; / \; (E_{wj}/E_{wn}),\qquad(1.1)$$

where E_{ij} is exports of commodity j by country i, w is the set of countries, and n is the set of all commodities. A country is said to have a comparative advantage in commodity j if RCA is greater than 1 and to have a comparative disadvantage in j if RCA is less than 1.

The DRC, as stated by Bruno (1972), is defined as follows:

$$d_j = \frac{-\sum_{s=2}^{m} \overline{f_{sj}} v_s}{u_j - \overline{m}_j},\qquad(1.2)$$

where d_j is the DRC of product j, m is the number of primary factors and n the number of products; v_s is the accounting (shadow) price for the sth primary factor ($s = 1$ is the foreign exchange), f_{sj} is the difference between the marginal dollar revenue of commodity j (u_j) and the (marginal) dollar import requirements for the unit production of commodity j (m_j), and a *bar* represents the total (direct and indirect) primary factors of production. The DRC directly measures a country's comparative advantage in a product and is particularly valuable in determining whether it makes economic sense for the government of an import-dependent country to spend money to foster exports that generate foreign exchange or to support import replacement that conserves foreign exchange. The DRC is a widely used index of economic efficiency in restrictive trade regimes.

An index value of less than 1 indicates that the cost of the domestic resources used to produce a unit of the product is less than the potential foreign exchange earnings from exporting the product, that is, the country has a comparative advantage in that product, and there is a rationale for the government to foster the export of the product. A DRC of greater than 1 indicates that the cost of the domestic resources used to produce the good for the domestic market is more than the foreign exchange required to import the good, that is, the country does not have a comparative advantage in the product, and the government should not be supporting import-substitution policies for it. It should be noted that the DRCs (and RCAs) are calculated on an ex post basis according to the existing resource endowment and policies. Policy reforms could change the DRC value over time. In industries that pass the DRC test, whether for exports or import substitution, integrated value chain studies can map the constraints to policy recommendations and identify what it will take for the government to promote the expansion of the identified industries.

For new products, latent comparative advantage, identified using the growth identification and facilitation framework, can pinpoint industries that are likely to be consistent with a country's comparative advantage (Lin and Monga 2010).

The framework postulates that, while a country's endowments (its infrastructure, for example) determine its comparative advantage at a given time, they can change if a country grows rapidly (that is, the country's comparative advantage becomes dynamic) (Lin 2009a). Some dynamically growing industries will lose their comparative advantage as the economy's endowment structure upgrades. These sunset industries will become the sunrise industries of countries in which the income levels are lower and in which the endowments are less capital intensive (that is, those countries will have a latent comparative advantage in these endowments). Over time, mastering the production of the simplest light manufactures such as T-shirts can open the door to a comparative advantage in more sophisticated light manufactures, but not without a corresponding upgrading of industry skills (Lin 2009b, 2010).

The approach we recommend for the identification of specific opportunities in manufacturing is a practical one (Dinh and others 2013). The government should let the private sector explore and undertake all initiatives with regard to product selection and markets. The role of the government at that stage is to provide the private sector with basic support in the form of infrastructure and other public goods. Once these initiatives prove successful, government support can become substantial and can vary from providing finance and training to offering land in industrial parks. This approach is consistent with the limited resources of Zambia, and it relies on market forces to bear the risks and to leverage the government support.

The Potential for Light Manufacturing in Africa

Many African countries have all the inputs needed for a competitive light manufacturing sector: a comparative advantage in low-wage labor, abundant natural resources sufficient to offset lower labor productivity relative to Asian competitors, privileged access to high-income markets for exports, and, in most cases, a sufficiently large local or regional market to allow emerging producers to develop capabilities in quick-response, high-volume production and quality control in preparation for breaking into highly competitive export markets.

This report proposes that these countries should follow the course pioneered by a succession of Asian countries by accelerating the realization of latent comparative advantage in segments of light manufacturing in which specific, feasible, sharply focused, low-cost policy interventions can deliver a quick boost to output, productivity, and, perhaps, exports, opening the door to expanded entry and growth.

Growing Markets Inside and Outside Africa

In recent years, four factors have opened new markets for Africa's light manufacturing firms:

- More rapid economic growth has expanded the size of the domestic market for manufactures in most countries. New markets thus offer new opportunities.

- Foreign investors and aid agencies are investing in manufactures destined for foreign markets. Examples include the U.S. Agency for International Development's technical assistance to Zambian farmers.
- For globally competitive light manufacturing firms in Sub-Saharan Africa, the market is the world. In 2005, the United States established new trade preferences under the African Growth and Opportunity Act, granting Zambian products exceptionally favorable access to the United States, while the European Union took similar measures under the Cotonou Agreement. These trade preferences are critical to the success of African exporters in the global apparel market; without the preferences, these countries are uncompetitive with efficient global exporters in markets in the European Union and the United States (World Bank 2011).[10]
- Regional integration within Africa increases the attractiveness of regional markets. Thus, Tanzania's and Zambia's participation in regional trade agreements has opened up new markets.

China's Growing Labor Cost Disadvantage

Chinese products have penetrated almost every corner of the global market. China supplied 18 percent of the combined value of the market imports in the European Union and the United States in 2004 and 35 percent in 2008. China is an inevitable competitor for Sub-Saharan African light manufacturing exports to these markets.

But the capacity of coastal Chinese firms to outperform rivals in low-income countries on both price and quality has begun an irreversible process of decline for labor-intensive light industry manufactures. The depletion of China's large pool of less highly skilled workers and rapid cost increases, particularly in wages and nonwage labor expenses, have begun to price many of China's coastal export firms out of global markets for these products. Some of the displaced production will shift to China's inland provinces, but new manufacturing clusters are also arising in Bangladesh, Cambodia, and other countries.

Rising wages, the stiffening enforcement of labor and environmental regulations, the gradual expansion of costly safety net provisions, and the prospect of increases in the international value of China's currency mean that China's comparative advantage in exports of labor-intensive manufactures will continue to erode, and the erosion could even accelerate. This prospect creates an opportunity for Sub-Saharan African countries to jump-start structural changes that hold the promise of delivering large and sustained increases in output, exports, employment, productivity, and incomes. China's efforts to limit the upward drift of its currency have contributed to substantial domestic inflation, spurring wage demands and hastening the erosion of cost advantages in labor-intensive manufactures.

This opens an entry point for other low-wage producers that can learn to compete, including firms based in Zambia. But low-income South Asia, East Asia, and the Middle East and North Africa will be hot contenders for newly available slices of the global market. The challenge facing Sub-Saharan African firms is whether they can compete with firms in Bangladesh and Nepal, as well as Cambodia, the Lao People's Democratic Republic, and Vietnam, which have low wages and large pools of less skilled labor. But even a small slice of the global apparel market would create millions of higher-productivity and higher-wage jobs in Sub-Saharan Africa.

Previous Policy Prescriptions: An Intimidating To-Do List

Past studies that reviewed the constraints on the expansion of light manufacturing in Sub-Saharan Africa came up with staggeringly long lists that implied that no feasible set of policy adjustments could make these countries attractive to investors. Most frustrating about these lists is the implication that, unless all the shortcomings are fixed, the sector cannot grow.

Yet, other economies have managed to expand the production and export of light manufactures without first resolving all the constraints currently observed in Sub-Saharan Africa. Visitors to China in the mid-1970s and early 1980s were appalled at the low product quality (sewing machines that leaked oil onto the fabric, as well as electric motors that failed in hot, humid weather); the passive management (one manager at a large plant insisted that he did not know the unit cost of his product; another manager asked to explain the presence of numerous idle workers, said "if we didn't employ them, where would they go?"); administrative confusion (would-be investors left the Xiamen Special Economic Zone in disgust after managers failed to provide stable prices for land, electricity, or water); delays in moving merchandise through customs and port facilities; lackadaisical attitudes toward customer needs; and on and on.

Emerging manufacturers in Zambia must, of course, compete with today's Chinese firms, not with the much weaker Chinese enterprises of the 1980s. But, as noted above, powerful market forces have begun to undermine the competitive advantage of China's well-established coastal centers of labor-intensive manufacturing. This process, which visitors to the region have been pointing out for at least the last five years, reflects irreversible forces that seem certain to intensify.

As China's coastal producers of apparel, leather products, and other labor-intensive manufactures experience a continuing squeeze on profitability, they will either shift to other lines of business or move to the interior, to other Asian countries (such as Bangladesh and Cambodia), or—as suggested in this report—to African countries such as Tanzania and Zambia.

The recommendations of this report, based on intensive study of specific sectors in Zambia, draw on the experience of countries such as China and Vietnam, which have managed to build thriving light industries despite the handicaps of problematic initial conditions. The logic underlying these recommendations is simple and direct.

While it will be difficult for new African manufacturers to match the price and quality advantages of well-established market leaders in China's coastal regions, the gradual erosion of the competitive advantage of Chinese firms is creating fresh opportunities. Initially, African firms would be able to build up their share of the domestic sales of labor-intensive manufactures and then, with the accumulation of skills, experience, and financial strength, enter global markets in competition with new entrants from China's interior and from countries such as Bangladesh and Cambodia, the economies of which suffer from some of the same difficulties and constraints now visible in Tanzania, Zambia, and their neighbors. As in China and Vietnam, introducing incentives to recruit foreign entrepreneurs and attract foreign direct investment can accelerate the process and expedite the pace of entry into global markets.

The approach proposed in this report is to use intensive study of individual light industry sectors to identify a concrete package of specific, feasible, and inexpensive policy initiatives that can maximize Zambia's opportunity to jump-start the growth of production, employment, and exports.

The experience of China and East Asian countries shows that development prospects benefit from macroeconomic stability and from a business environment that encourages rather than obstructs entrepreneurial initiative. Recent improvements confirm that, for many African countries, the macroeconomic environment is no longer a critical constraint to industrial growth. In fact, Tanzania and Zambia are among several African countries that, over the past decade, have improved macroeconomic conditions (less inflation, lower deficits) and provided opportunities to private entrepreneurs. International experience also shows that manufacturing can expand rapidly despite challenging institutional arrangements. For example, China did not introduce laws protecting the property rights of private businesses until after 2000, and clearly specified implementation mechanisms are missing. Private businesses still have little access to bank lending or to formal financial markets.

Although Sub-Saharan African countries usually rank low on many components of the World Bank's doing business index, evidence from the quantitative and enterprise surveys undertaken for this project shows that Sub-Saharan African firms do not face notably different conditions from those of their counterparts in China (Harrison, Lin, and Xu 2011). These constraints may be important, but, as Chinese experience demonstrates, they need not constitute impassable barriers to expansion and upgrading.

Resolving Critical Constraints in the Most Promising Sectors

The favorable observations about macroeconomic circumstances and the business environment in Sub-Saharan Africa notwithstanding, accelerating structural transformation requires that several substantial obstacles be overcome, particularly those that involve finance, infrastructure (electricity, roads), governance, and human capital. Because African governments cannot relax all these constraints at once, this report proposes a different approach to jump starting light manufacturing. Focusing value chain analysis and other analyses on a handful of carefully chosen sectors, picking reasonable benchmarks, and aiming for price competitiveness make it possible to trim the long list of constraints into a few leading constraints in each of the most promising sectors. Such priorities make the exercise more manageable, the policy actions more precise, and the sequencing easier. They also make it possible to exploit the potential for light manufacturing by identifying the few most critical steps Sub-Saharan African governments can take to remove these constraints in the most promising sectors first.

This two-stage study advances the understanding of what is required to establish light manufacturing by laying out specific actions built on successful experiences in low-income countries. It accomplishes the following:

- Identifies specific sectors as potential candidates for start-ups
- Pinpoints constraints that have obstructed manufacturing in these sectors
- Highlights concrete policy measures that can remove these constraints and create opportunities for private domestic or foreign entrepreneurs to initiate light manufacturing operations

This approach builds on the work of Hausmann, Rodrik, and Velasco (2005), who visualized development as a continuous process of specifying binding constraints that limited growth, formulating and implementing policies to relax the constraints, securing modest improvements in performance, and then renewing growth by identifying and pushing against the factors limiting expansion in the new environment. It is also consistent with the new structural economics approach (Lin 2010), which views economic development as a process requiring the continuous introduction of new and better technologies in existing industries and the upgrading of labor- and resource-intensive industries to new, more capital-intensive industries.

Following Hausmann, Rodrik, and Velasco, our approach emphasizes that development begins somewhere, but not everywhere. In Africa, as in China, applying limited funding and administrative personnel to implement a set of sharply focused reforms holds the promise of establishing new clusters of production, employment, and, eventually, exports without first resolving economy-wide problems of land acquisition, utility services, skill shortages, administrative shortcomings, and the like.

Notes

1. Also see "About Light Manufacturing in Africa," Data and Research, World Bank, Washington, DC (accessed March 5, 2012), http://go.worldbank.org/0PHUIVOUT0.
2. World Development Indicators (database), World Bank, Washington, DC, http://data .worldbank.org/data-catalog/world-development-indicators.
3. A discussion of why these five countries and five analytical tools have been selected, together with detailed results, may be found in Dinh and others (2012) and is also available at "Book: Light Manufacturing in Africa; Targeted Policies to Enhance Private Investment and Create Jobs," Data and Research, World Bank, Washington, DC, http://go.worldbank.org/ASG0J44350.

4. See Enterprise Surveys (database), International Finance Corporation and World Bank, Washington, DC, http://www.enterprisesurveys.org.

5. This section has been prepared by Vandana Chandra.

6. Following the United Nations (UN 2009) *International Recommendations for Industrial Statistics 2008*, this report defines manufacturing as section C of the International Standard Industrial Classification of All Economic Activities, Revision 4: "the physical or chemical transformation of materials, substances or components into new products. . . . The materials, substances or components transformed are raw materials that are products of agriculture, forestry, fishing, mining or quarrying or products of other manufacturing activities. . . . Assembly of the component parts of manufactured products is considered manufacturing. This includes the assembly of manufactured products from either self-produced or purchased components." Within manufacturing, light industry usually refers to labor-intensive, consumer-oriented products, such as the five product sectors specified in this book.

7. For the data, see UN Comtrade (United Nations Commodity Trade Statistics Database), Statistics Division, Department of Economic and Social Affairs, United Nations, New York, http://comtrade.un.org/db.

8. Panagariya (2008, 286) further argues as follows: "greater expansion of unskilled-labor-intensive sectors still offers greater scope for the employment of unskilled labor. . . . No evidence is available showing that shifts in technologies have narrowed the relative differences between unskilled-labor intensities across sectors. As for the magnitude of expansion, the world markets offer huge scope for it. If policies are right, India could replace China as the manufacturing hub of unskilled-labor-intensive products of the world."

9. We are grateful to Professor Howard Pack for this point.

10. The recent severe deterioration in Madagascar's apparel production after the removal of its eligibility under the African Growth and Opportunity Act is a case in point.

References

Balassa, Bela. 1965. "Trade Liberalization and 'Revealed' Comparative Advantage." *Manchester School of Economic and Social Studies* 33 (2): 92–123.

Bruno, Michael B. 1972. "Domestic Resource Costs and Effective Protection: Clarifications and Synthesis." *Journal of Political Economy* 80 (1): 16–33.

Chenery, Hollis. 1980. "Interactions between Industrialization and Exports." *American Economic Review* 70 (2): 281–87.

Commission on Growth and Development. 2008. *The Growth Report: Strategies for Sustained Growth and Inclusive Development*. Washington, DC: World Bank. https://openknowledge.worldbank.org/handle/10986/6507.

Corden, W. Max. 1984. "Booming Sector and Dutch Disease Economics: Survey and Consolidation." *Oxford Economics Paper* 36 (3): 359–80.

Corden, W. Max, and J. Peter Neary. 1982. "Booming Sector and Deindustrialization in a Small Open Economy." *Economic Journal* 92 (368): 825–48.

Dinh, Hinh T., Vincent Palmade, Vandana Chandra, and Frances Cossar. 2012. *Light Manufacturing in Africa: Targeted Policies to Enhance Private Investment and Create Jobs*. Washington, DC: World Bank. http://go.worldbank.org/ASG0J44350.

Dinh, Hinh T., Thomas G. Rawski, Ali Zafar, and Lihong Wang. 2013. *Tales from the Development Frontier: How China and Other Countries Harness Light Manufacturing to Create Jobs and Prosperity*. With contributions by Eleonora Mavroeidi, Xin Tong, and Pengfei Li. Washington, DC: World Bank.

Harrison, Ann E., Justin Yifu Lin, and L. Colin Xu. 2012. "Performance of Formal Manufacturing Firms in Africa." In *Performance of Manufacturing Firms in Africa: An Empirical Analysis*, edited by Hinh T. Dinh and George R. G. Clarke, 27–46. Directions in Development Series. Washington, DC: World Bank. https://openknowledge .worldbank.org/handle/10986/11959.

Harrison, Ann E., and Andrés Rodríguez-Clare. 2010. "Trade, Foreign Investment, and Industrial Policy for Developing Countries." In *The Handbook of Development Economics*, edited by Dani Rodrik and Mark R. Rosenzweig, *Handbooks in Economics*, Vol. 5, 4039–214. Amsterdam: Elsevier North Holland.

Hausmann, Ricardo, Dani Rodrik, and Andrés Velasco. 2005. "Growth Diagnostics." John F. Kennedy School of Government, Harvard University, Cambridge, MA.

Kuznets, Simon. 1959. *Six Lectures on Economic Growth*. Glencoe, IL: The Free Press.

Lin, Justin Yifu. 2009a. "DPR Debate: Should Industrial Policy in Developing Countries Conform to Comparative Advantage or Defy it? A Debate between Justin Lin and Ha-Joon Chang." *Development Policy Review* 27 (5): 483–502.

———. 2009b. *Economic Development and Transition: Thought, Strategy, and Viability*. Cambridge: Cambridge University Press.

———. 2010. "New Structural Economics: A Framework for Rethinking Development." Policy Research Working Paper 5197, World Bank, Washington, DC.

Lin, Justin Yifu, and Célestin Monga. 2010. "Growth Identification and Facilitation: The Role of the State in the Dynamics of Structural Change." Policy Research Working Paper 5313, World Bank, Washington, DC.

Naughton, Barry. 2007. *The Chinese Economy: Transitions and Growth*. Cambridge, MA: MIT Press.

NBS (China, National Bureau of Statistics). 2003. *China Labor Statistical Yearbook 2003*. Beijing: China Statistics Press.

Panagariya, Arvind. 2008. *India: The Emerging Giant*. London: Oxford University Press.

Seers, Dudley. 1964. "The Open Mechanism of an Open Petroleum Economy." *Social and Economic Studies* 13 (2): 233–42.

Thirlwall, A. P. 1983. "A Plain Man's Guide to Kaldor's Growth Laws." *Journal of Post Keynesian Economics* 5 (3): 345–58.

UN (United Nations). 2009. *International Recommendations for Industrial Statistics 2008*. Statistical Papers Series M 90, ST/ESA/STAT/SER.M/90. New York: Statistics Division, Department of Economic and Social Affairs, United Nations. http://unstats .un.org/unsd/EconStatKB/Attachment387.aspx.

U.S. Department of Commerce. 1995. *Engines of Growth: Manufacturing Industries in the U.S. Economy*. Washington, DC: Office of Business and Industrial Analysis, Economics and Statistics Administration, U.S. Department of Commerce.

World Bank. 2011. *Kaizen for Managerial Skills Improvement in Small and Medium Enterprises: An Impact Evaluation Study*. Vol. 4 of *Light Manufacturing in Africa: Targeted Policies to Enhance Private Investment and Create Jobs*. Washington, DC: World Bank. http://go.worldbank.org/4Y1QF5FIB0.

CHAPTER 2

Economic Background

Introduction

A peaceful, democratic country with enormous economic potential, Zambia has a rich endowment of natural resources (fertile land and large water, mineral, and forestry resources). From independence in 1964 to the early 1990s, Zambia followed an economic policy of pervasive state intervention in factor and product markets and large-scale state ownership of productive assets (World Bank 2000). For many years, the effects of these policies on the economy were masked by the revenue generated by copper production and exports. But, when world copper prices fell, the inefficiencies of Zambia's interventionist economy became more evident as domestic incomes and output came under increasing downward pressure. The government tried to offset the decline in copper earnings by borrowing heavily abroad, but the economic decline continued. Incomes fell rapidly over the 1980s, while the country became heavily indebted.

The new government that took office in 1991 launched a program of economic stabilization and liberalization designed to reverse the economic decline and put Zambia on a path of sustainable growth. Prices were decontrolled and subsidies eliminated; inflation was brought down considerably; market forces were allowed to determine the exchange rate and interest rate; quantitative restrictions on imports were eliminated; and the tariff structure was compressed and simplified. State enterprise monopolies were ended; crop marketing was liberalized; and a far-reaching privatization program made good progress.

The Promising Economic Growth since 2000

Zambia has recorded promising economic growth since 2000 thanks to these new economic policies, improving copper prices, and substantial donor assistance, including debt relief. The gross domestic product (GDP) rose an average of 5.6 percent a year over 2000–10, and inflation has been held to single digits. Economic expansion has been particularly robust in mining (10.6 percent) and construction (15.2 percent). Growth averaged 4.2 percent in manufacturing and 4.8 percent in services (table 2.1). Meanwhile, dominated by smallholder family

Table 2.1 Sectoral Composition of GDP Growth, Zambia, 2000–10

percent

Sector	Annual average growth rate	Share of GDP	
	2000–10	2000–02	2008–10
Agriculture	2.3	16.1	12.6
Industry	—	26.1	32.7
Mining and quarrying	10.6	7.1	9.2
Manufacturing	4.2	10.6	9.5
Food, beverages, and tobacco	6.1	59.6	68.7
Textile and leather products	−8.9	17.2	6.1
Wood and wood products	5.2	7.4	8.2
Paper and paper products	8.7	2.8	3.7
Chemicals, rubber, and plastic products	4.4	8.5	8.8
Fabricated metal products	2.1	2.2	2.0
Electricity	3.3	3.0	2.4
Construction	15.2	5.4	11.6
Services	4.8	58.7	54.7
GDP, total	5.6	100.0	100.0

Source: Central Statistical Office of Zambia.

Note: — = not available; GDP = gross domestic product.

farms, agriculture has grown at 2.3 percent a year over the period. Despite the high overall growth, almost two-thirds of Zambians still live in poverty, and, on most measures of social welfare, rural people persistently do less well than urban dwellers.

During the first decade of the 2000s, there were some changes in the structure of production. The share of industry, broadly defined to include mining, manufacturing, electricity, and construction, increased from 26 percent of GDP in 2000–02 to almost 33 percent in 2008–10. However, the share of manufacturing fell from 10.6 to 9.5 percent. The combined share of food, beverages, and tobacco in manufacturing went up from 59.6 to 68.7 percent, while the share of textile and leather products fell from 17.2 to 6.1 percent.

Among exports, diversification away from copper has been slow. Noncopper exports have grown at an average rate of 14 percent in current dollar terms, but copper still constitutes about 70 percent of total exports, largely because of high international prices. This is worrisome because mining dependence has led the country to a decline in per capita incomes and to several crises in the last 50 years. To resolve the current problems, Zambia has to begin a structural shift in production from mining and subsistence farming to modern agriculture, agroindustry, tourism, and light manufacturing. This shift is inevitable if Zambia is to lift its people out of poverty and create employment for the 200,000 young people who enter the labor force each year.[1]

Zambia's Potential and the Main Constraints to Competitiveness

Zambia has not fully exploited its latent comparative advantage in resource-based light manufacturing industries. To maintain its growth momentum and share the benefits of growth more broadly, Zambia will need to use its untapped natural resources more effectively. The government has ambitious plans to realize this objective, described in its Vision 2030 proposals and the Sixth National Development Plan for 2011–15 (MCTI 2006; MOF 2011). A key area of priority is resource-based light manufacturing, where the emphasis is on spreading economic opportunities in a balanced way across all segments of the population and regions of the country through increased access to skills, resources, and markets and improved connectivity and integration.

The goal of our study is to assist the government in formulating the policy reforms needed to achieve its ambitious plans. In particular, the study aims to assess the key features, strengths, and weaknesses of five light manufacturing sectors (apparel, leather products, wood products, metal products, and agribusiness), identify the main constraints in these sectors that prevent Zambian companies from taking advantage of market opportunities, and suggest actions to overcome these constraints. Promoting light manufactures will help Zambia diversify production and exports away from copper and smallholder agriculture, shifting the economy toward a more diversified economic profile that encompasses higher–value added light manufacturing industries.

This is an especially crucial time for Zambia to act. China's comparative advantage in light manufactures is slowly eroding because of the steeply rising cost of labor, land, and regulatory compliance in that country. As China graduates from some light manufactures, Zambia will have an opportunity to increase its own share in domestic and international markets.

Some barriers, such as limited access to credit and lack of entrepreneurial and technical skills, afflict all five sectors. Others are specific to individual sectors. Programs, appropriately packaged and sequenced, need to address both types of barriers. Implementing the proposed cross-sectoral policies simultaneously in all manufacturing sectors may not be feasible initially because this would strain limited institutional and administrative capacity and financial resources. Focusing on the selected sectors to generate marked impacts could make it easier to expand the approach to other areas later. The sector-specific constraints are discussed in the chapters on individual sectors (chapters 5–9). While our broader study covers five countries (China, Ethiopia, Tanzania, Vietnam, and Zambia), China is considered Zambia's main competitor in domestic, regional, and global markets for light manufacturing products, as evidenced by the flood of Chinese products into these markets. China has also been identified as one of the two main competitors (together with South Africa) in the quantitative surveys of Zambian firms undertaken as part of our research (Fafchamps and Quinn 2012). If Zambia can compete successfully with China, it should be able to compete with other countries in the five selected products. The rest of this chapter looks at Zambia's current advantages and disadvantages compared with China.

Advantages

Zambia's substantial potential in expanding its light manufacturing industries is based on four key advantages, as follows:

- *Low labor cost:* Nominal wages are lower in Zambia than in China for both skilled and unskilled labor (table 2.2). The wages in the informal sector, where more than 80 percent of the labor force work, are much lower than the wages in the formal sector. Clarke (2012) reports that, in 2008, the monthly labor costs in a median unregistered micro, small, and medium enterprise was less than $30 per worker, about one-fourth of the corresponding labor costs in a median formal manufacturing firm. Labor productivity is similar (slightly higher in some sectors and slightly lower in others), except in wood products, where it is substantially lower in Zambia (see table 3.2 in chapter 3). This gives Zambia a considerable labor cost advantage. However, this advantage is wiped out by other cost elements.

- *Rich natural resources:* Zambia has a rich supply of raw materials such as cotton, hides and skins, wood, minerals, and agricultural products for the production of intermediate goods such as yarn, cloth, leather, timber, and metal sheets and rods. This provides an opportunity for the development of an integrated domestic supply chain in light manufacturing. However, the supply chain is now broken.

Table 2.2 Quantitative Results of Company Surveys, China and Zambia, 2010
percent unless otherwise indicated

Characteristic	China	Zambia
Average monthly wage (US$)		
Skilled	305–399	284–364
Unskilled	197–278	157–208
Share of companies with owners with more than partial secondary education	90	50
Share of production workers without any education	0	37
Share of companies providing in-kind benefits		
Housing	82	15
Subsidized meals	80	77
Share of companies experiencing power outages	36	70
Share of companies with membership in business associations	45	20
Share of companies receiving no outside assistance during start-up		
Technical advice	9.7	42.9
Financing	32.6	64.9
Share of companies exporting part of their output	39	5
Share of companies that borrowed from banks and nonbank institutions	60	8
Annual average interest paid	4.7	21.0

Source: GDS 2011.

- *Growing domestic market:* Zambia's significant and broadbased economic growth—averaging 5.6 percent over the past 10 years—and its growing middle class are creating strong demand for light manufacturing products. However, that demand in the light manufactures in which Zambia has a latent comparative advantage is being met largely by imports. Zambia can replace part of these imports by strengthening its competitiveness.

- *Access to foreign markets:* Zambia has duty- and quota-free access to the main developed-country markets for almost all its manufactured products under the European Union's Everything but Arms Initiative, the U.S. African Growth and Opportunity Act, and the Generalized System of Preferences of the other industrialized countries. Also, as a member of the Common Market for Eastern and Southern Africa and the Southern African Development Community, Zambia trades in regional markets on preferential terms. However, Zambia cannot take advantage of these opportunities because supply-side constraints prevent it from producing competitively.

The gradual erosion of China's cost advantage in light manufactures provides a good opportunity for Zambia to improve its competitiveness and increase its market share in domestic and global markets. The steeply rising cost of land, regulatory compliance, and labor—both wages and benefits—in China has begun to erode that country's cost advantage, particularly in the coastal export manufacturing centers. Some Asian countries (Bangladesh and Cambodia) are lining up to fill the gap. Zambia will need to seize this opportunity to upgrade its light manufacturing sectors.

Some Disadvantages

To make the most of this opportunity, Zambia must overcome several disadvantages in its policy environment relative to China. According to the findings of firm surveys in China and Zambia (see Fafchamps and Quinn 2012 for details):

- The average size of small and medium companies is substantially larger in China: companies with 2–20 workers make up 23 percent of this group in China and 67 percent in Zambia.
- Chinese companies have more well-educated owners: 90 percent of owners have more than a partial secondary education in China; the share is 50 percent in Zambia.
- Production workers in China have a higher level of educational attainment: the share of production workers without any education is negligible in China, but 37 percent in Zambia.
- Chinese companies provide greater in-kind benefits. For example, 82 percent of surveyed Chinese companies provide housing, and 80 percent provide subsidized meals. The shares in Zambia are 15 and 77 percent, respectively.
- Chinese companies experience fewer power outages: 36 percent of Chinese companies reported power outages compared with 70 percent in Zambia.

- Membership in sectoral associations is more prevalent among Chinese companies: 45 percent of companies in China compared with 20 percent in Zambia.
- Chinese companies receive more assistance from family members and others for start up, including ideas, technical assistance, and financing.
- Chinese companies face less import competition: 94 percent of Chinese companies report no import competition, while the corresponding share is only 53 percent among Zambian companies. This discrepancy is partly explained by China's undervalued exchange rate.
- Chinese companies export a larger share of their output: 39 percent in China compared with 5 percent in Zambia.
- Chinese companies have better access to finance: 60 percent of companies in China report they borrowed from a bank, nonbank financial institution, or government agency; the share is only 8 percent among Zambian firms.
- Chinese companies borrow at a lower interest rate: an annual average rate of about 4.7 percent in China compared with 21.0 percent in Zambia.

These weaknesses are elaborated in the following chapters, and recommendations on policies to address these weaknesses are discussed.

Note

1. Zambia's labor force is currently estimated at 5 million and has been growing at 4 percent per year.

References

Clarke, George R. G. 2012. "Manufacturing Firms in Africa." In *Performance of Manufacturing Firms in Africa: An Empirical Analysis*, edited by Hinh T. Dinh and George R. G. Clarke, 47–86. Directions in Development Series. Washington, DC: World Bank.

Fafchamps, Marcel, and Simon Quinn. 2012. "Results of Sample Surveys of Firms." In *Performance of Manufacturing Firms in Africa: An Empirical Analysis*, edited by Hinh T. Dinh and George R. G. Clarke, 139–211. Washington, DC: World Bank.

GDS (Global Development Solutions). 2011. *The Value Chain and Feasibility Analysis; Domestic Resource Cost Analysis*. Vol. 2 of *Light Manufacturing in Africa: Targeted Policies to Enhance Private Investment and Create Jobs*. Washington, DC: World Bank. http://go.worldbank.org/6G2A3TFI20.

MCTI (Zambia, Ministry of Commerce, Trade, and Industry). 2006. *Vision 2030: "A Prosperous Middle-Income Nation by 2030."* Lusaka.

MOF (Zambia, Ministry of Finance and National Planning). 2011. *Sixth National Development Plan 2011–2015: "Sustained Economic Growth and Poverty Reduction."* Lusaka: MOF.

World Bank. 2000. "Report and Recommendation of the President of the International Development Association to the Executive Directors on a Proposed Fiscal Sustainability Credit of SDR 105.5 Million (US$140 Million Equivalent) to the Republic of Zambia." Report, Washington, DC.

CHAPTER 3

The Business Environment for Firms

Introduction

In Zambia, market access is not a binding constraint to export growth in the five identified product industries: apparel, leather products, wood products, metal products, and agribusiness. The binding constraints are on the supply side: Zambia cannot compete in its own market or in international markets and cannot take advantage of its latent comparative advantage because it cannot produce competitively in these industries. This supply problem arises because of both cross-sectoral and sector-specific factors. This chapter reviews the former, including the real exchange rate and trade policy. Chapters 5–9 discuss the sector-specific issues.

The packaging and sequencing of the cross-sectoral and sector-specific reforms will vary across industries and over time, depending on location-specific conditions and binding constraints in each sector. A key question is whether Zambia should implement the cross-sectoral policies in all light manufacturing sectors at the same time. Doing so could strain the country's institutional and administrative capacity and financial resources so much that all sectors suffer. More effective would be to exert a strong impact in the selected sectors before applying the policies more broadly.

The Macroeconomic Framework

Macrostability

Zambia's economy has always been affected by variations in the price of copper, the country's main commodity export. Figures 3.1 and 3.2 show the evolution of world copper prices and of per capita incomes in Zambia over the last 50 years.

The volatility in the world price of copper and Zambia's dependence on this commodity for exports and income imply that the Zambian economy is frequently susceptible to external shocks. If the Zambian authorities maintain a fixed exchange rate regime, the transmittal of these shocks could lead to a crisis in the balance of payments unless copper revenues are managed efficiently.[1] On the other hand, a flexible exchange rate regime will keep the economy

Figure 3.1 World Copper Price, 1960–2011

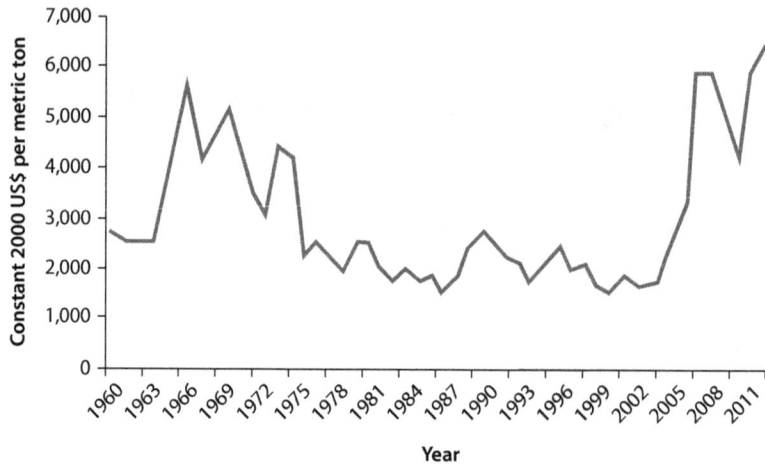

Source: World Bank 2012.

Figure 3.2 GDP per Capita, Zambia, 1960–2011

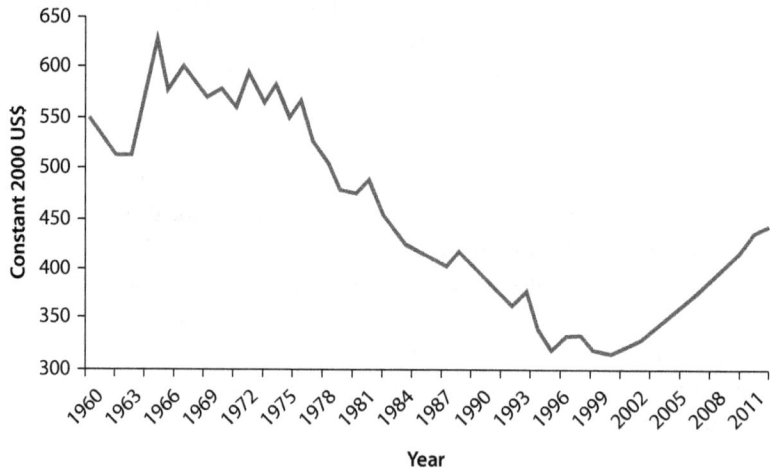

Source: World Bank 2012.
Note: GDP = gross domestic product.

insulated from these shocks, but at the expense of manufacturing production and exports because the producers of these goods face wide variations in the real exchange rate, and this affects profitability and business planning (figure 3.3). At the same time, Zambia's capital account has been liberalized for a number of years, thus increasing the magnitude and speed of exchange rate volatility. In the course of nine months, between June 2008 and April 2009, the kwacha depreciated by 74 percent and then appreciated by 12 percent.

In the longer run, the best way to avoid this macroinstability would be to diversify the economy away from mineral production and exports toward

Figure 3.3 Exchange Rate, Zambia, 2000–11

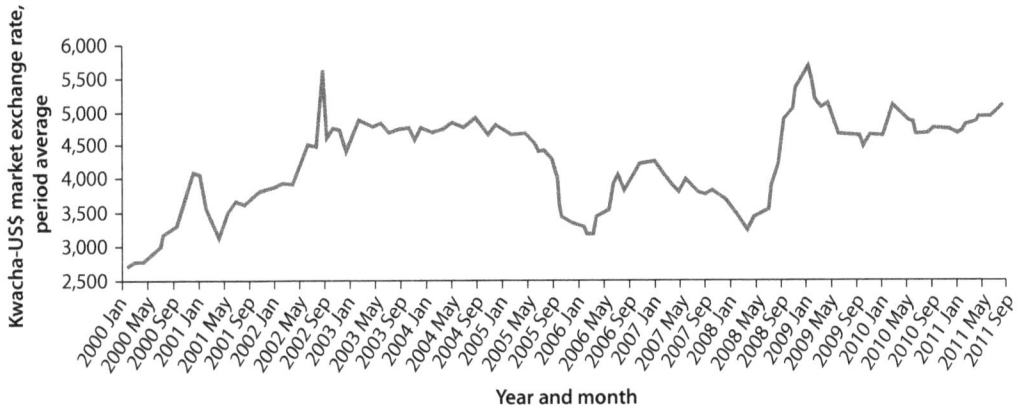

Source: IMF 2012.

agriculture, agroindustry, tourism, and light manufacturing. In the short and medium term, it may be necessary for the government to establish a stabilization fund to hold any surplus above the long-run trend in the world copper price as savings for a rainy day. This would allow the monetary authorities to maintain the exchange rate at a stable rate.[2] Some interventions in the foreign exchange market is needed to reduce the volatility of the exchange rate. In addition, it is important to maintain a strict fiscal and monetary policy stance to keep inflation and interest rates at a low and stable level that is conducive to business expansion.

Exchange Rates

Exchange rates are an important determinant of international competitiveness. Changes in real effective exchange rates contribute to changes in the competitiveness of export sectors across countries.

Zambia has a free-floating exchange rate that follows the fortunes of the copper mining industry. Like many other resource-based economies, Zambia is at risk of both currency volatility (which makes it more difficult for businesses to make investment and operational decisions) and long-term currency appreciation (the Dutch Disease, which reduces the competitiveness of non–resource-based export sectors of the economy).[3]

The real effective exchange rate of the Zambian kwacha appreciated considerably between 2000 and 2006 before leveling off following the global financial crisis, while the Chinese yuan remained fairly stable (figure 3.4; table 3.1). The Zambian authorities have acknowledged that appreciation of the kwacha has had a negative impact on export competitiveness in recent years (Kalyalya 2008).

At the moment, the real effective exchange rate of the kwacha seems to be close to the equilibrium level, and there are no grounds for expecting it to fall against the yuan and other major competitive currencies. This limits Zambia's

Figure 3.4 Changes in Real Effective Exchange Rates, Yuan and Kwacha, 2000–11

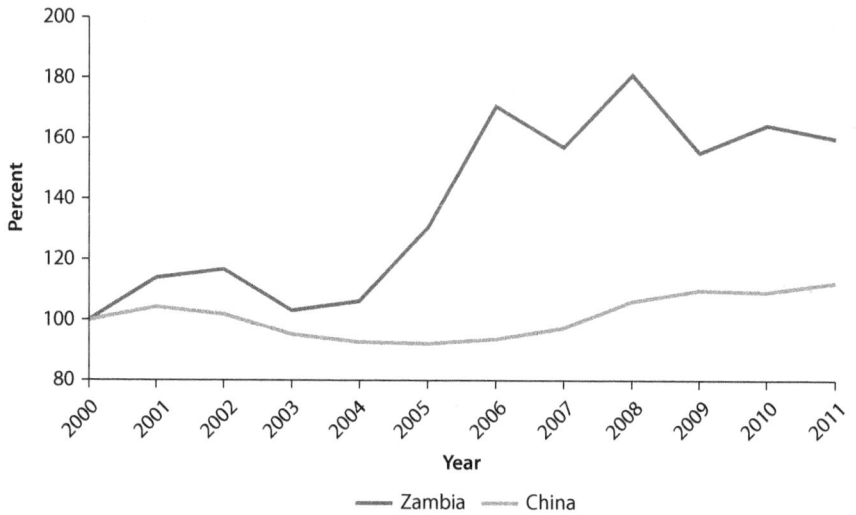

Sources: World Bank compilation from data in International Financial Statistics (database), International Monetary Fund, Washington, DC, http://elibrary-data.imf.org/FindDataReports.aspx?d=33061&e=169393; World Economic Outlook Database, International Monetary Fund, Washington, DC, http://www.imf.org/external/pubs/ft/weo/2011/02/weodata/index.aspx.

Table 3.1 Real Effective Exchange Rate Index, Yuan and Kwacha, 2001–10
2000 = 100

Currency	2001	2002	2003	2004	2005	2006	2007	2008	2009	2010	2011
Chinese yuan	104.3	101.9	95.2	92.6	92.1	93.6	97.3	106.2	109.8	109.3	112.3
Zambian kwacha	113.9	116.7	103.1	106.2	130.5	170.6	157.2	181.0	155.3	164.4	160.0

Sources: World Bank compilation from data in International Financial Statistics (database), International Monetary Fund, Washington, DC, http://elibrary-data.imf.org/FindDataReports.aspx?d=33061&e=169393; World Economic Outlook Database, International Monetary Fund, Washington, DC, http://www.imf.org/external/pubs/ft/weo/2011/02/weodata/index.aspx.

opportunity to gain competitiveness over other exporters in the sector (GDS 2011; IMF 2010). Furthermore, as long as Zambia's economy is dominated by natural resource industries, the exchange rate is likely to follow developments in the copper mining industry, as in the past. Zambia's manufacturing (and other non–resource-based export industries) may therefore be at risk from currency volatility and appreciation. To counter these adverse effects, Zambia could establish a sterilization fund that would manage the inflows of foreign currency by investing some of the foreign currency inflows in the nontradable sectors such as infrastructure.

The international debate over whether China's currency is over- or undervalued and the implications for international trade and competitiveness are well known. China has faced rising international pressure to allow its currency to appreciate to correct global trade imbalances. Appreciation of the yuan would be expected to reduce the competitiveness of China's manufacturing (and other) exports (Chen and Dao 2011).

World Bank research suggests that there has been no overall real appreciation in the yuan relative to the U.S. dollar since the late 1990s, despite productivity growth, because of offsetting monetary policies (Kuijs 2009). In the traded goods sector, however, labor productivity has grown by more than 9 percent a year in China compared with only slightly above 2 percent among its main competitors, resulting in a cumulative difference of more than 60 percent over an eight-year period (IMF 2010). This would tend to boost China's international competitiveness. However, rising wages and other labor costs, a diminishing labor surplus, and the long-run decline in the share of the working population are likely to make it increasingly difficult for China to continue to keep a competitive edge, at least at the low end of manufactured goods. A recent report of the United Nations Conference on Trade and Development observes that "rising wages [in China] amount to a real appreciation of the yuan" (UNCTAD 2011, 21).

Export Incentives and Trade Facilitation

Zambia's trade regime and trade facilitation arrangements have an antiexport bias. The duty drawback system is too complex and poorly implemented, leading to confusion about coefficients and to payment delays; customs administration is cumbersome; valuation methods for imports are arbitrary; standards infrastructure is weak; and transportation costs are high (World Bank 2005). These arrangements do not provide adequate incentives to expand Zambia's exports and diversify them away from copper toward the many light manufacturing industries in which Zambia has a latent comparative advantage.

The government has taken steps to strengthen the incentives system and improve trade facilitation to reduce the cost of export activities:

- It has lowered import duties on capital goods and intermediate products. Following an internal review of the duty drawback system in 2010, the government decided to streamline the system by working out the coefficients with exporters, strengthening the duty drawback unit in the Zambia Revenue Authority, and processing drawback claims electronically.

- The government asked the World Bank to update the Diagnostic Trade Integration Study with a view to preparing an export diversification strategy for Zambia. The work is expected to start soon.

- Under the donor-financed Private Sector Development Reform Program, the government has prepared a comprehensive national quality policy and implementation plan to guide the establishment of appropriate infrastructure (organizations, structures, and systems for metrology, standards, and accreditation) compatible with international norms (MCTI 2011a, 2011b). This is an important initiative aimed at bringing Zambia into compliance with international health and safety norms and technical standards, vital for gaining access to developed-country markets. The European Union is providing technical assistance for implementation through its Export Development Program.

- Under the Private Sector Development Reform Program, the government is also streamlining customs administration and establishing one-stop border posts with neighboring countries. There are three border post initiatives: Chirundu, at the border with Zimbabwe (largely operational); Nakonde, at the border with Tanzania (a memorandum of understanding has been signed with the government of Tanzania); and Kasumbalesa, at the border with the Democratic Republic of Congo (planned; a memorandum of understanding has not yet been signed). The European Union is supporting this initiative under its Private Sector Development Program.

These are important reform initiatives for reducing the antiexport bias. Some were begun several years ago, but implementation has been slow. Continuing donor support is needed to accelerate the implementation of these reforms.

Wages and Productivity

Zambia's greatest assets are its large pool of low-wage, less-skilled workers (tables 3.2 and 3.3). While labor productivity in the average firm is low, good management and technical assistance could raise it to the level in the most well managed firms. The low skill requirements of light manufacturing sectors make it possible to train unskilled workers quickly and cheaply in only a few weeks.[4] While this advantage is unlikely to be permanent, it provides an opportunity to promote new industries that may, like China's, prosper for decades and create millions of productive jobs, much as East Asia did early on and as Bangladesh and Vietnam are doing today.

Table 3.2 Monthly Wages in Light Manufacturing, Five Countries
US$

Product	Labor type	China	Vietnam	Ethiopia	Tanzania	Zambia
Polo shirts	Skilled	311–370	119–181	37–185	107–213	n.a.
Leather loafers	Skilled	296–562	119–140	41–96	160–200	—
Wood chairs	Skilled	383–442	181–259	81–119	150–200	200–265
Crown corks	Skilled	265–369	168–233	181–	—	–510
Dairy milk	Skilled	177–206	—	30–63	150–300	106–340
Milled wheat	Skilled	398–442	181–363	89–141	200–250	320–340
Average	Skilled	305–399	154–235	77–131	153–233	284–364
Polo shirts	Unskilled	237–296	78–130	26–48	93–173	—
Leather loafers	Unskilled	237–488	78–93	16–33	80–140	—
Wood chairs	Unskilled	206–251	85–135	37–52	75–125	100–160
Crown corks	Unskilled	192–265	117–142	89–	—	–342
Dairy milk	Unskilled	118–133	31–78	13–41	50–80	54–181
Milled wheat	Unskilled	192–236	78–207	26–52	100–133	131–149
Average	Unskilled	197–278	78–131	35–53	80–130	157–208

Source: GDS 2011.
Note: The upper values for crown corks (bottle caps) are not available for Ethiopia. The lower values for crown corks are not available for Zambia. — = not available; n.a. = not applicable.

Table 3.3 Labor Productivity in Light Manufacturing, Five Countries

Labor productivity	China	Vietnam	Ethiopia	Tanzania	Zambia
Polo shirts, pieces per employee per day	18–35	8–14	7–19	5–20	—
Leather loafer, pieces per employee per day	3–7	1–6	1–7	4–6	—
Wooden chair, pieces per employee per day	3.0–6.0	1.0–3.0	0.2–0.4	0.3–0.7	0.2–0.6
Crown corks, pieces per employee per day x 1,000[a]	13–25	25–27	10	—	201
Dairy farming, liters per employee per day	23–51	2–4	18–71	10–100	19–179
Wheat processing, tons per employee per day	0.2–0.4	0.6–0.8	0.6–1.9	1.0–22.0	0.6–1.6

Source: GDS 2011.
Note: Data on wheat processing are taken from a sample of small enterprises in the five countries; — = not available.
a. Crown cork (bottle cap) production in Zambia is fully automated.

Adjusted for productivity, wages in Zambia (in the formal sector) are similar to wages in China, although they are higher in Zambia than in other low-income countries because of high inflation in Zambia (GDS 2011). But other costs are considerably higher in Zambia than in China, most notably interest rates and the exchange rate. The question is how to get these three key prices right—wages, interest rates, and the exchange rate—so as to exploit Zambia's latent comparative advantage.

To move the labor productivity of the average firm toward current domestic best practice does not require costly training for all workers. The chief ingredient is new or improved enterprise management, together with targeted technical assistance. The impact of such changes can already be seen in the Zambian shoe industry. Detailed research conducted as part of our study of light manufacturing in Africa demonstrates the feasibility of achieving substantial management upgrades in small firms through inexpensive, short-term training (World Bank 2011). Once begun, upgrading can become self-sustaining as word spreads of the tangible benefits accruing to early participants in training seminars. Attracting new investors, particularly overseas entrepreneurs who can bring production and marketing experience in the target industries, as well as financial resources and technical expertise, can accelerate industrial expansion and structural change.

Given the high proportion of the labor force in the informal sector, the huge gap in wages between the formal and informal sectors (chapter 2), and the fact that wages in Zambia are relatively higher than wages in other low-income countries, the case may be made for a review of labor laws and regulations governing the formal labor market. There are three main options. One is to revise labor laws and regulations openly, including minimum wage laws, with the aim of making them competitive with laws and regulations, not in neighboring countries, but in countries that are competing in the domestic market (for example, China and India). This approach could be politically difficult to implement, however, because it would mean lowering formal sector wages. Another option is to let current labor laws and regulations expire. A third option is to limit initially the scope of labor reforms to exporters (as Mauritius did) and to key industries or locations (such as industrial parks or economic zones).

Access to Credit

Access to credit has been identified as the most binding constraint on small companies in developing countries (Dinh, Mavridis, and Nguyen 2012). Only around 2 percent of micro, small, and medium enterprises have access to credit products (Clarke and others 2010). Impeding access to credit are lack of collateral, high interest rates, and productivity that is too low to attract or service loans.[5]

Small companies in Zambia are served by three types of financial institutions. The first is microfinance institutions, introduced in 2000. Most of the 24 microfinance institutions are commercial; there are only a few social microfinance institutions run by nongovernmental organizations. Most of the credit is in the form of loans to civil servants that are backed by salaries.[6] These loans vary from K 100,000 ($20) to K 10 million ($2,000). Part of these salary-backed loans are thought to be used by relatives of the borrowers to finance micro and small businesses. The number of microfinance clients is estimated at 200,000–250,000, or 20–25 percent of the number of commercial bank customers (World Bank and IMF 2009). Social microfinance institutions have much more limited reach, at about 50,000 customers. Total microfinance lending is around K 1 billion ($200 thousand), and the recovery rate is more than 95 percent. Most microfinance institutions on-lend loans they receive from commercial banks, although some institutions have started to collect deposits. They receive lines of credit from the Development Bank of Zambia (DBZ).

A second financial institution is the Citizens Economic Empowerment Commission (CEEC), which was established in 2006 to support targeted segments of the population. One of the major activities of the CEEC is to extend working capital and investment credit to small companies from the Citizens Economic Empowerment Fund. The fund had initial capital of K 200 billion ($40 million), and K 40 billion ($8 million) more was allocated in the 2012 budget. More than 1,600 people have benefited from the fund since it was launched in 2008. The upper limit for loans was initially K 50 million ($10,000), but it was recently reduced. Loans are of two types: trade loans (90 days) and project loans (one, three, or five years). All loans have a grace period of up to two months. Collateral requirements have recently been introduced for CEEC loans. (Machinery is accepted as collateral.) According to CEEC management, the loan recovery rate is 42 percent. Allocations seem to be made on political grounds, without appropriate credit risk assessments. Because the CEEC has no expertise in financial activities, it would make sense to transfer the operations of the Citizens Economic Empowerment Fund to a specialized institution, such as a microfinance institution.

The third institution is the DBZ, a public bank. It also extends microcredits of K 5 million ($1,000) to small companies. The DBZ plans to establish a dedicated fund for micro, small, and medium businesses. It has already created the Zambia

Enterprise Development Fund Ltd., owned jointly with the Zambia Development Agency (ZDA), to finance investment projects. The DBZ will manage the fund. The fund will have initial capital of $15 million, $5 million of which has been provided by the ZDA; the DBZ is contributing $1.5 million. The fund will focus mainly on agricultural firms because about 70 percent of micro, small, and medium firms are in agriculture.

One of the key reasons for the limited access to finance is lack of collateral. Establishing and managing an effective credit guarantee scheme are therefore essential for improving access.[7] The DBZ created a partial credit guarantee scheme in 2009 under the donor-supported Financial Sector Development Program with initial capital of $1.6 million. The scheme provides guarantees for 60 percent of the value of loans to small and medium businesses. So far, the offtake has been poor because of administrative weaknesses. The capital base is also small. The DBZ recently reached an agreement with three commercial banks (International Commercial Bank, Standard, and Madison Finance Company) and two microfinance institutions to promote this facility. Improving offtake requires scaling up capital, strengthening the implementation capacity of the DBZ, launching an awareness campaign, and working closely with commercial banks and microfinance institutions.

Zambia also has a privately managed credit reference bureau and plans to establish a collateral registry under the Financial Sector Development Program, though no action has yet been taken.[8]

Entrepreneurship, Management, and Technical Skill Training

The government recognizes that inadequate entrepreneurship, management, and technical skill training are key constraints to growth in Zambia and has several programs to address them (Clarke and others 2010). The Technical Education, Vocational, and Entrepreneurship Training Authority, established in 1998, is the main government institution charged with upgrading needed skills. Operating under the Ministry of Science, Technology, and Vocational Training, it manages 24 large institutions offering one- to three-year programs to people of all ages. Students pay a fee for training. These schools turn out about 5,000 graduates every year. These supply-driven programs are often poorly matched to the skills that industry needs because curricula are not adapted quickly enough to the changing structure of individual industries and the technologies they use. Graduates work mainly in the informal sector, where they are self-employed. The training authority also accredits more than 300 private vocational training institutions, which offer mainly two- and three-week business management and information technology skills.

To facilitate entrepreneurship, management, and technical skill training, particularly among smaller companies, the ZDA plans to work through private business development service providers that have expert trainers in a wide range of fields accredited by the ZDA. The development policy implementation plan for micro, small, and medium businesses suggests a need to improve the capacity of these business development service providers (MCTI 2010a). The ZDA will facilitate training by these providers through local branches of the Small-Scale Industries Association of Zambia, the Zambia Chamber of Small and Medium Business Associations, the Zambia Federation of Associations of Women in Business, and the Zambia Farmers Union. The ZDA will charge the companies a small facilitation fee for these services. The ZDA support of business development service providers will include capacity building, bookkeeping, financial management, project and business plan preparation, credit application assistance, and other topics.

The government of Finland is also planning to develop a business incubator program for smaller companies in Zambia.

There are two kaizen programs in Zambia. One is a Japan International Cooperation Agency technical assistance program for the ZDA under which three Japanese trainers teach the kaizen method of management to smaller companies at no cost. The other kaizen program is conducted jointly by the Zambia Association of Manufacturers and the Kaizen Institute of Africa (an Indian company based in Mauritius). This is a demand-driven program aimed mainly at larger companies. Training is conducted whenever there are enough applications (usually 20–25). After training, follow-up conferences are held to assess the results. Two conferences have been held so far. The Kaizen Institute for Africa and the Zambia Association of Manufacturers are planning a Kaizen College in Zambia similar to the one in Kenya.

No evaluations have been carried out on the scale and impact of these programs to determine if they meet the needs of manufacturing industries. The programs should be reviewed and evaluated as part of an effort to identify specific recommendations for improving training capacity in the country.

Institutional Support and Policy Coordination

A sectoral strategy and an implementation plan prepared in collaboration with all stakeholders are essential for establishing a vision for the sector; setting priorities and detailed policies; identifying areas for government intervention, including sector-specific (and location-specific) infrastructure (refrigerated storage facilities, abattoirs, industrial clusters, market centers, training facilities and programs, leveling the playing field, and so on); and coordinating the efforts of all stakeholders, including donors.

Until recently, Zambia did not have sectoral strategies to guide investors. Sectoral policies were largely ad hoc, reactive, and uncoordinated. With donor support under the Private Sector Development Reform Program II, the government completed preparation of a commercial, trade, and industrial policy in 2009 covering 2010–24 (MCTI 2010b). Setting out broad objectives for Zambian industry, the program identifies six priority sectors: processed food, textiles and garments, engineering products, gemstones, leather and leather products, and wood and wood products. With the assistance of the Japan

International Cooperation Agency, the government is preparing a sectoral strategy for the engineering products sector.

Institutional support for industry, particularly for micro, small, and medium firms, is weak and uncoordinated in Zambia. ZDA's Micro and Small Enterprise Division will be responsible for the implementation of the development policy for micro and small firms, in coordination with other concerned agencies (ministries and other government departments, business associations, financial institutions, and so on) under the leadership of the Ministry of Commerce, Trade, and Industry.[9] The capacity of the ZDA is too limited for such a critical responsibility. The ZDA has seven regional offices, but each office is staffed by a single person.

The ZDA intends to implement the development policy in collaboration with the local offices of the Zambia Chamber of Small and Medium Business Associations, the Small-Scale Industries Association of Zambia, the Zambia Federation of Associations of Women in Business, and the Zambia Farmers Union. These organizations have district-level affiliate associations, but their capacity is also weak.

It is advisable to launch an immediate capacity assessment of all the agencies involved, particularly the ZDA and the ZDA Micro and Small Enterprise Division, and take appropriate measures to scale up their implementation capabilities. The role of the Zambia Association of Manufacturers could also be strengthened. Unless the capacity of the ZDA Micro and Small Enterprise Division, the sector associations, training institutions, and other relevant organizations is substantially upgraded, the policy will not be effectively implemented. In particular, the capacity of the Zambia Chamber of Small and Medium Business Associations and the Small-Scale Industries Association of Zambia should be greatly strengthened because they are to be the key agencies in promoting the interests of the sector, interacting with government agencies, and representing the sector with the Zambia Business Forum, the apex representative of the business community in Zambia.

Economic Zones and Industrial Parks

In line with the Export Processing Zone Act of 2001, the government established the Zambia Export Processing Zone Authority in 2003 to build and operate export processing zones. Because of a lack of clarity about its responsibilities, the Authority never became fully operational.

Following the establishment of the ZDA, the act on export processing zones was repealed, and, in 2006, a new law introduced the concept of a multifacility economic zone. These economic zones are being administered by the Investment Promotion and Privatization Division of the ZDA. There are two main differences between the multifacility economic zones and the abandoned export processing zones: the multifacility zones are open to all companies, including those producing for the domestic market, and they are developed and operated mainly by private companies.

Light Manufacturing in Zambia • http://dx.doi.org/10.1596/978-0-8213-9935-4

Through statutory instruments, the Ministry of Commerce, Trade, and Industry has earmarked five locations for multifacility economic zones and one for an industrial park: Chambishi, Lumwana, Lusaka East, Lusaka South, Sub-Sahara Gemstone Exchange, and Roma Industrial Park (a smaller version of a multifacility economic zone, with an area of at least 15 acres). Only the Chambishi zone has opened. It is being developed and operated by the Zambia-China Economic and Trade Cooperation Zone Company. There are 14 Chinese companies active in the zone; these produce products and services for the Chinese-operated mines in the region. They have created more than 3,500 local jobs. The other multifacility zones are in various stages of development. With the exception of the Lusaka South zone, all are to be developed by private companies.

The new law reflects a flexible approach to zone development. Depending on the licensing agreements with the operating companies, part of the infrastructure and social facilities in and around the zones will be developed by the government. Companies operating in the zones benefit from substantial fiscal, institutional, administrative, and social incentives.

Various types of export processing zones played an important role in facilitating industrial upgrading and export promotion in East and South Asia and Latin America in the 1980s and 1990s. Africa's experience with such zones over the past two decades has been less successful. With the exception of Mauritius and some scattered successes in Kenya, Lesotho, and Madagascar, African export processing zones have failed to attract substantial investment or promote exports (Farole 2011). The main factors contributing to the failure include poor strategic planning (a mismatch with comparative advantage); poor locational choices; insufficient investment in infrastructure; poor implementation capacity; and a lack of authority, high-level support, or policy stability. Zambia's new zone policy appears to have been influenced by these African experiences.

Notes

1. The Chilean and Norwegian experiences show that a balance of payments crisis can be averted if revenues from mineral exports are saved.

2. The monetary authorities can keep the exchange rate at a stable rate provided the exchange rate is monitored in a timely fashion to avoid any balance of payment crisis.

3. For example, the well-respected Behre Dolbear index ranks Zambia in the bottom three of 25 mining countries in terms of currency stability (Behre Dolbear 2011).

4. Survey results for light industries show that "in Ethiopia and China, 85–90% [of firms] report that it takes at most four weeks for new workers to be fully trained" (Fafchamps and Quinn 2012, 16).

5. Real estate and land are normally accepted as collateral. The Development Bank of Zambia (DBZ) has also started to accept machinery and household effects as collateral.

6. Employees at private companies are served largely by commercial banks.

7. Partial credit guarantee schemes are widely used by developed and developing countries to support the growth of smaller businesses. Bilateral and multilateral donors have supported the creation of such schemes. The Financial Sector Assessment Program for Zambia endorses an initiative whereby the DBZ would administer a guarantee scheme as a second-tier activity (World Bank and IMF 2009).

8. These financing arrangements are part of Zambia's financial system, and reforms should be undertaken in the context of an overall financial sector reform program. For a detailed analysis and recommendations, see World Bank and IMF (2009).

9. The ZDA, a semiautonomous institution, was established in 2006 and became operational in January 2007 with the amalgamation of five statutory bodies that had operated largely independently to support economic development in Zambia (the Zambia Investment Center, the Export Board of Zambia, the Zambia Export Processing Zones Authority, the Small Enterprise Development Board, and the Zambia Privatization Agency). The ZDA also has a one-stop shop to facilitate quick business start-ups. Appointed by the Ministry of Commerce, Trade, and Industry, the ZDA board comprises members from the public and private sectors and civil society organizations. The chairperson and vice chairperson are appointed from the private sector. The head office is in Lusaka, and there are regional offices in Chipata, Kasama, Kitwe, Livingstone, Mansa, Mongu, and Solwezi. ZDA has five organizational divisions: Investment Promotion and Privatization, Micro and Small Enterprise Development, Export Promotion and Market Development, Research Planning and Policy, and Corporate Services. It has 21 sectoral specialists.

References

Behre Dolbear. 2011. "2011 Ranking of Countries for Mining Investment or 'Where Not to Invest'." Behre Dolbear Group, London. http://www.dolbear.com/announcements/asdf.

Chen, Ruo, and Mai Dao. 2011. "The Real Exchange Rate and Employment in China." IMF Working Paper WP/11/148, International Monetary Fund, Washington, DC.

Clarke, George R. G., Manju K. Shah, Marie Sheppard, Juliet Munro, and Roland V. Pearson, Jr. 2010. "Zambia Business Survey: The Profile and Productivity of Zambian Businesses." Zambia Business Forum, Private Sector Development Reform Program (Ministry of Commerce, Trade, and Industry), FinMark Trust, and World Bank, Lusaka.

Dinh, Hinh T., Dimitris A. Mavridis, and Hoa B. Nguyen. 2012. "The Binding Constraint on Growth of Firms in Developing Countries." In *Performance of Manufacturing Firms in Africa: An Empirical Analysis*, edited by Hinh T. Dinh and George R. G. Clarke, 87–138. Directions in Development Series. Washington, DC: World Bank.

Fafchamps, Marcel, and Simon Quinn. 2012. "Results of Sample Surveys of Firms." In *Performance of Manufacturing Firms in Africa: An Empirical Analysis*, edited by Hinh T. Dinh and George R. G. Clarke, 139–211. Directions in Development Series. Washington, DC: World Bank.

Farole, Thomas. 2011. *Special Economic Zones in Africa: Comparing Performance and Learning from Global Experiences*. Directions in Development Series: Trade. Washington, DC: World Bank.

GDS (Global Development Solutions). 2011. *The Value Chain and Feasibility Analysis; Domestic Resource Cost Analysis*. Vol. 2 of *Light Manufacturing in Africa: Targeted*

Policies to Enhance Private Investment and Create Jobs. Washington, DC: World Bank. http://go.worldbank.org/6G2A3TFI20.

IMF (International Monetary Fund). 2010. *Zambia: 2009 Article IV Consultation; Third Review under the Three-Year Arrangement under the Poverty and Reduction and Growth Facility, and Request for Modification of Performance Criteria.* IMF Country Report 10/17, Washington, DC. http://www.imf.org/external/pubs/cat/longres.aspx?sk=23539.0.

———. 2012. *International Financial Statistics.* April. Washington, DC: Statistics Department, IMF.

Kalyalya, Denny H. 2008. "Current Issues in the Management of the Exchange Rate and Inflation." Presentation to the Economics Association of Zambia, Lusaka, June 17.

Kuijs, Louis. 2009. "China through 2020: Macroeconomic Scenario." World Bank China Research Paper 9, World Bank, Beijing.

MCTI (Zambia, Ministry of Commerce, Trade, and Industry). 2010a. *The Micro, Small and Medium Enterprise Development Policy Implementation Plan, 2010–14.* Lusaka.

———. 2010b. *Commercial, Trade and Industrial Policy.* Lusaka.

———. 2011a. *The National Quality Policy.* Lusaka.

———. 2011b. *The National Quality Policy Implementation Plan, 2011–2015.* Lusaka.

UNCTAD (United Nations Conference on Trade and Development). 2011. *Trade and Development Report, 2011: Post-crisis Policy Challenges in the World Economy.* Geneva, Switzerland: UNCTAD.

World Bank. 2005. *Zambia: Diagnostic Trade Integration Study (Trade Component of Private Sector Development Program for Zambia).* Washington, DC.

———. 2011. *Kaizen for Managerial Skills Improvement in Small and Medium Enterprises: An Impact Evaluation Study.* Vol. 4 of *Light Manufacturing in Africa: Targeted Policies to Enhance Private Investment and Create Jobs.* Washington, DC: World Bank. http://go.worldbank.org/4Y1QF5FIB0.

———. 2012. *World Development Indicators.* April 24. Washington, DC: World Bank.

World Bank and IMF (International Monetary Fund). 2009. *Financial Sector Assessment Program: Zambia FSAP Update.* Washington, DC.

CHAPTER 4

Light Manufacturing in Zambia

Introduction

With an average annual growth rate of 3.3 percent and an average contribution to gross domestic product (GDP) of 10.2 percent, Zambia's manufacturing sector did not achieve its targets of 7.5 percent annual growth and a 15 percent contribution to GDP over the period covered by the Fifth National Development Plan (2006–10). The share of manufacturing in total exports averaged 2.1 percent, and the contribution of the sector to total employment rose from 1.3 percent in 2005 to 3.2 percent in 2008.

Nonetheless, from the country's perspective, manufacturing is "a pivot of economic development" (MOF 2011, 133). The Sixth National Development Plan (SNDP) emphasizes the potential for "locally abundant natural resources" to serve as a strong foundation for value added, export-focused, technology-based manufacturing with backward and forward links to economic growth, exports, and employment creation (MOF 2011, 135). Zambia's goal is to develop, by 2015, "a diversified and competitive export-led value adding manufacturing sector that will contribute 12.5 percent to GDP" (MOF 2011, 135).

The results of the analysis conducted for this report suggest that light manufacturing could add value to Zambia's natural resources and, potentially, help achieve the aspirations of the national development plans. Chapters 5–9 summarize the potential and the constraints in each of five light manufacturing sectors (apparel, leather products, wood products, metal products, and agribusiness) and recommend steps to improve competitiveness.[1]

Three main results emerge from the analysis:

1. *Zambia has the potential to expand production and perhaps become regionally competitive in several light manufacturing sectors.* While exports of some low-value, high-volume products such as furniture and simple metal products may not be feasible, there is enough local demand for these products if they are competitive with imports. The country's labor cost advantage—relative to Asia, wages are low in local goods firms in some sectors—and comparative

advantage in natural resource industries such as agriculture, livestock, and forestry can be leveraged to increase the competitiveness of locally produced light manufacturing goods on domestic and regional markets. International competitiveness may also be achievable over time in some sectors.

2. *Issues in key input industries are, collectively, the main constraints on Zambia's competitiveness in light manufacturing.* Examples include the lack of good-quality leather and the high cost of wheat, steel, and wood inputs. Input costs represent more than 70 percent of total production costs in light manufacturing. The other important constraints are poor trade logistics and poor access to skills, equipment, finance, and industrial land. These last constraints affect smaller firms in particular.

3. *A few specific interventions would accomplish much in the effort to address the main constraints.* These key interventions include liberalizing output and input markets in agriculture; removing import tariffs on the main light manufacturing inputs; facilitating the access to rural land among good practice investors in agriculture, livestock, and forestry; facilitating the entry of leading investors along the value chain; developing plug-and-play industrial parks; improving trade logistics; and deploying targeted technical and managerial training programs.[2]

The rest of this chapter sets the context for the analysis by providing a brief overview of Zambia's light manufacturing sector. In chapters 5–9, we present our detailed findings for each of the five light manufacturing sectors. In chapter 10, we synthesize the results and discuss how to implement a reform program taking into account institutional, fiscal, and political economy issues.

Overview of Light Manufacturing

Despite the small size of the economy, Zambia produces a fairly wide range of light manufactured goods. The country's legacy of state-led industrialization saw the creation of many large firms and continuing demand by the mines for a variety of industrial products. More recently, a vibrant informal trading and manufacturing sector has arisen, together with new formal sector firms. Some products are exported, including to neighboring countries such as the Democratic Republic of Congo, but, for the most part, Zambia's light industry sector competes with imports, mainly from Asia (particularly China and India) and South Africa.

All five sectors considered in this study use raw materials—the output of the first stage of the value chain—produced in Zambia, but a large part of that output is currently exported. Thus, the production chain is broken after the first stage. A share of the raw material is processed domestically (the middle stage of the value chain), but the processing technology is outdated, and the quality is inferior to the quality of imported products. In some cases, the higher-quality intermediate inputs are exported. The final products (the final stage of the value chain) that are produced with the locally processed inferior intermediate inputs lack quality and modern design features and cannot compete in global markets or with imports in domestic markets.

Cotton is a good example. Zambia produces good-quality cotton, but three-quarters of the cotton is exported after ginning (largely to South Africa), leaving only a quarter for the first intermediate stage of the value chain (spinning). Higher-quality yarn is exported, and the rest is woven into cloth in the second intermediate stage. The yarn and the fabric produced domestically lack quality and cannot support a competitive apparel market. Domestically produced fabric is used in the production of low-value or niche products mainly for the domestic market (for mineworkers, school uniforms, and so on). Produced from low-quality intermediate inputs, domestically produced apparel cannot compete with imported new or, especially, second-hand clothing in quality or price.

Linking the supply chain is a key issue in the medium and long terms. The middle stage of the production process is more intensive in technologies and skills. Therefore, linking the supply chain requires attracting foreign direct investment in the middle phase of the chain to produce for local and export markets. By linking the supply chain in some sectors, Zambia could capture more value from its raw materials, create more employment, and generate more foreign exchange (see chapters 1 and 7). China and many East Asian countries have followed a successful industrial strategy whereby they first devote their own investment resources to the assembly of finished products to build up an economic base before investing in the intermediate stages of production to link up the supply chain.

Moreover, vertical integration may not be possible immediately in some products. For example, in leather products, the priority may be to upgrade the livestock sector by addressing skin diseases, such as ectoparasites, and improving the quality of raw materials (hides and skins). Complete integration is not possible in any sector. Some raw materials could be exported, and some intermediate goods will need to be imported, depending on market opportunities and the specific final products targeted for local production. In any event, the export ban on inputs and the tax on raw materials should be eliminated.

The Size of Manufacturing Enterprises

Zambia classifies manufacturing companies as micro, small, medium, and large based on the number of employees, the annual revenue, and capital investment (excluding land and buildings) (table 4.1). Capital investment is delineated according to whether the firm is engaged in manufacturing or trade and services. All enterprises are also classified by legal status. Any company not registered with the Registrar of Companies is classified as an informal company. To qualify as micro, small, or medium, an enterprise must meet the total investment criteria, together with at least one other criterion.

According to the Ministry of Commerce, Trade, and Industry, about 97 percent of manufacturing enterprises are micro or small, and more than 80 percent

Table 4.1 Company Classification by Size, Zambia

Size	Employees, total	Annual turnover, kwacha, millions	Total investment, kwacha, millions	Legal status
Micro	Up to 10	Up to 150	80	Majority in informal sector
Small	11–50	151–250	81–200	Most in informal sector
Medium	51–100	251–300	201–500	Most in formal sector
Large	101 or more	301 or more	501 or more	All in formal sector

Source: MCTI 2009.

are informal. The industry is thus characterized by a small number of large, for-mal enterprises and a vast majority of micro, small, and informal enterprises. This has important implications for the promotion of light manufacturing industries because the policy environment affecting micro, small, and medium enterprises is different from that affecting larger enterprises. A key objective of Zambia's industrialization program is to assist smaller firms to grow and integrate with larger companies through initiatives to ensure the access of the smaller firms to markets and services, such as business incubation, entrepreneurship and technical skills training, finance, technology transfer, institutional support, clustering and industrial parks, and so on.

To tackle the constraints that hinder the transformation of smaller firms, the government issued the 10-year micro, small, and medium enterprise development policy in 2009 (MCTI 2009). The government also prepared a policy implemen-tation plan for 2010–14, the first five-year segment, which coincides with the SNDP period (MCTI 2010a). The government sees the development strategy and the recently adopted commercial, trade, and industrial policy as important instru-ments for achieving the broader national development goals outlined in the Vision 2030 proposals and the national development plan (MCTI 2006, 2010b). One of these goals is to diversify production and exports away from the copper industry. The barriers to growth identified by the micro, small, and medium enter-prise development policy encompass limited access to markets, technology, finance, and infrastructure facilities, including business premises; limited entrepre-neurial, management, and technical skills; an inadequate regulatory system; and excessive competition from cheap, unregulated imports.

Responsibility for much of the implementation is assigned to the Zambia Development Agency (ZDA). The ZDA's Micro and Small Enterprise Division is responsible for establishing strategic partnerships for policy implementation with other concerned agencies inside and outside government. The Ministry of Commerce, Trade, and Industry will monitor and evaluate performance. The ZDA board will establish a subcommittee as an advisory body, with 11 members drawn from the public sector, the private sector, and business associations.

The development policy and the companion implementation plan provide a well-conceived vision for the sector and a detailed action plan to implement the vision. The main challenge concerns the implementation and interagency coordination capacity of the government.

Market Segmentation[3]

Broadly speaking, Zambia's market comprises three main segments. One is the informal sector market, which offer a wide range of products, many of them produced in small facilities in or close to the markets. These products are generally of low quality and include wooden and upholstered furniture, shoes, clothing, assorted hardware (for example, buckets, chicken feeders, and bars for windows and doors), spare parts, and mending and welding services. Some products are imported and traded locally, particularly donated secondhand clothing, which displaces much local production.[4] Some are produced by formal sector Zambian firms. Reportedly, the incidence of theft from formal sector factories is significant, implying that a portion of informally marketed products may be illicit. Zambian and imported products often compete; the former are usually (but not always) cheaper and of lower quality.[5] The owners of small informal sector firms tend to be indigenous Zambians who are at a disadvantage in accessing information; entrepreneurial, financial, and physical capital; and training.

Microproducers in this segment are generally outside the web of regulations that suffocate formal sector Zambian firms. While some enterprises produce for informal markets as a last resort, some are able to earn fairly good incomes, sometimes higher than they could receive if they were in the formal sector. Many of the more skilled workers seem to have learned their trades in Zambia's formal sector factories before being laid off or quitting, as happened in China in the early 1980s. They work hard and rely on basic capital equipment, sometimes homemade.

A second segment comprises formal sector outlets, which are at the higher end of the consumer market. Many of these firms are owned or operated by foreigners or by ethnic minority Zambians (especially Asians), often with good contacts in other countries. These outlets are frequently South Africa–based chains (for example, Shoprite, PEP) that are positioned in shopping malls and source their products from established suppliers. Apart from fresh food and some processed agricultural products, many of the goods these firms sell are made outside Zambia. Shoes and clothing, including items for children and items made of leather or cotton, two of Zambia's primary exports, are usually imported from Asia, while cookware, tableware, and utensils are imported from Asia or South Africa. The product variety and the links to global design and fashion distinguish these market segments. Allowing for the small size of the Zambian market, these products are of the sort that might be seen in shops in any middle-income country.

The Zambian products that are carried in this higher-end distribution segment of the market are all supplied by formal sector firms. In general, even if local industries produce similar goods (clothing, aluminum pots), they are not competitive. Zambian industry is therefore effectively locked out of this higher-end and potentially growing urban market.

The larger-scale production and marketing firms in construction materials and furniture distribution are part of this segment. They carry some Zambian products (high-end handmade hardwood furniture, doors, kitchens, and security bars, generally made to order; high-quality insulated electrical wire; roofing sheets), but many of their offerings are imported. These imports include cheaper furniture, often of particleboard veneer; other furniture imported in knocked-down kits from Asia; and higher-quality door and window fittings (often from South Africa). In some cases, Zambian products made in the informal sector compete with these items (security bars for windows and doors, wooden doors, furniture), but their inferior quality places them in a different market segment, which is similar to the situation in China in the 1980s.

A third segment is special orders placed by major buyers, such as the mines (for example, furniture, uniforms, safety boots), schools (uniforms, desks), government agencies and the military (uniforms, tents), and donors (blankets), a largely captive market for long-established formal sector Zambian suppliers, though some imports may also be involved. The items in this segment are largely standardized. There is an emphasis on stable quality, but there is little innovation in design. Many items are produced on old equipment—dating to an era before privatization and liberalization—that has not been replaced because the factories are already operating below capacity.

The rigid segmentation of markets in Zambia implies that policies to grow the manufacturing sector have to take into account the different constraints of these markets and that one possible way to raise productivity in the economy is to strengthen the weak backward and forward links among companies and among markets. The Citizens Economic Empowerment Commission was established partly to assist population groups that have not fully benefited from the economic progress achieved thus far. The commission runs several support programs, including financial assistance and the citizens reservation program. Under the micro, small, and medium enterprise development policy, the government is planning to set up industrial parks and clusters and business brokering and sub-contracting services to integrate companies and markets more effectively (MCTI 2009, 2010a).

It is tempting to conclude that Zambia should continue to rely on its mineral production and export sector, given the segmentation in local markets, the lack of a competitive alternative to imported products in the output of local light manufacturing industries in the formal sector, and the vast informal sector, with its limited economic scale and technology adaptation. Yet, it is mining that has been behind the steady decline in per capita incomes over the last half century. To achieve its vision of becoming a prosperous middle-income nation by 2030, Zambia must shift away from mining and subsistence farming toward a more diversified economy that encompasses higher–value added sectors such as light manufacturing (MCTI 2006). There is no other way to lift the population out of poverty and create employment for the 200,000 young people that enter the labor force each year.[6]

The next five chapters examine light manufacturing sectors that could offer opportunities for adding value in Zambia: the apparel, leather products, wood products, metal products, and agribusiness industries. Each chapter presents the potential of the sector, the binding constraints, and relevant recommendations.

Notes

1. All these are considered priority sectors by the government.

2. A duty drawback scheme is in place for manufacturing firms in sectors other than mining that export or intend to start exporting. However, firms producing for the domestic market (which is, in the medium term, likely to be the primary focus of many of the sectors covered in this report) do not benefit from this scheme.

3. This section is based on a contribution by Alan Gelb as part of a mission to Zambia in July 2009.

4. Retail and wholesale trade in Zambia has tended to be easier to undertake, more profitable, and less risky than manufacturing (Cardozo and others 2010). This has contributed to an increase in informal trading rather than manufacturing.

5. This is similar to the case of China today. China is the largest exporter of household appliances in the world, but the quality of many household appliances produced for the domestic market in China is lower than the quality of imports from firms in Germany, Italy, Japan, and the Republic of Korea.

6. Zambia's labor force is estimated at 5 million and has been growing at an average of 4 percent a year.

References

Cardozo, Adriana, Gibson Masumbu, Chiwama Musonda, and Gaël Raballand. 2010. "Growth, Employment, Diversification and the Institutional Context of Private Sector Development in Zambia." Draft working paper, World Bank, Washington, DC.

MCTI (Zambia, Ministry of Commerce, Trade, and Industry). 2006. *Vision 2030: "A Prosperous Middle-Income Nation by 2030."* Lusaka.

———. 2009. *The Micro, Small and Medium Enterprise Development Policy.* Lusaka.

———. 2010a. *The Micro, Small and Medium Enterprise Development Policy Implementation Plan, 2010–14.* Lusaka.

———. 2010b. *Commercial, Trade and Industrial Policy.* Lusaka.

MOF (Zambia, Ministry of Finance and National Planning). 2011. *Sixth National Development Plan 2011–2015: "Sustained Economic Growth and Poverty Reduction."* Lusaka: MOF.

CHAPTER 5

Textiles and Apparel

Introduction

In the 1980s, under an import-substitution development strategy that included high tariff protection and government subsidies, Zambia had a vibrant textile and garment sector with more than 140 companies employing over 25,000 Zambians (Chikoti and Mutonga 2002). A combination of macroeconomic shocks; major constraints in trade logistics, worker skills, and input costs; and the flooding of markets with secondhand goods greatly weakened and diminished the sector. When the government could no longer afford the subsidies and had to liberalize the trade regime following severe macroeconomic shocks, there were mass closings of garment factories and a scaling down of operations in the 1990s and the first decade of the 2000s.

Since then, the sector has been hurt by a volatile macroeconomic environment (in 2000–06; see chapter 3), including an overvalued exchange rate and a flood of cheap used and donated clothing that has had a deleterious effect on local industry; Zambia is one of the few countries in the world that permits unlimited imports of secondhand clothing. In addition to these external factors, several internal factors have contributed to the industry's demise, including the lack of a competitive input industry with reasonable prices, the use of obsolescent machinery, and the absence of skilled managers experienced with global markets. Poor access to working capital has also hindered industry expansion.

The Zambian textile and garment industry was unable to survive strong international competition, especially following the expiration of the Multi-Fiber Arrangement in 2005. As of mid-2012, the textile and garment sector consisted of an estimated 12 medium or large companies producing primarily niche products—such as school and industrial uniforms, protective clothing for the mining industry, and local ethnic garments—for the domestic and regional markets. The sector employs about 1,500 people, three-quarters of them men (in China and Vietnam, more than three-quarters are women). According to the Central Statistical Office of Zambia, the annual production of all apparel totaled less than 8,700 metric tons in 2009, 39 percent less than in 2007. Most fabric and finished products (including a large volume of secondhand clothing) are imported: in 2009, apparel imports totaled around $18.7 million, while exports totaled only about $0.3 million.[1]

Industries feeding into the apparel subsector are similarly weak. High-quality cotton is produced locally (approximately 73,000 tons were produced in the 2009/10 growing season), and all seed cotton is ginned in the country. The spinning industry is a major missing link: all the ginned output is exported, while the (small) textile industry imports yarn, and, in some cases, the apparel industry imports fabric.[2] The market and institutional support structure for cotton and cotton apparel in Zambia is outlined in figure 5.1.[3]

Sectoral Potential

Several factors limit the sector's competitiveness, and becoming competitive would require large gains in productivity (see below). Until then, the main opportunities for Zambia's apparel sector lie in producing low-value and niche products for the domestic and regional markets (where they would face less competition from Asian exporters), such as uniforms and protective and ethnic clothing, the current focus of Zambian production. Opportunities for import substitution are limited: domestically produced apparel is rarely a substitute for

Figure 5.1 The Cotton-to-Garment Market and Institutional Support Structure, Zambia

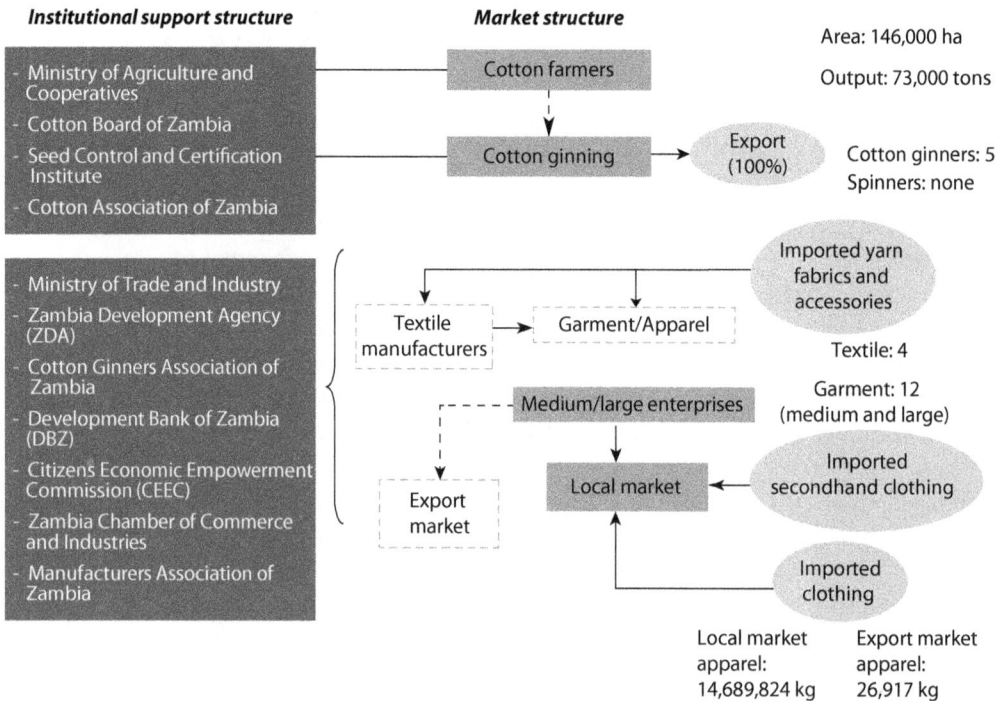

Source: GDS 2011.
Note: Dashed lines indicate a weak link, lack of organization, and areas where technical support is required to strengthen ties along the supply chain.

imports, especially considering the strong competition from secondhand clothing. Zambia receives preferential access to markets in the European Union and the United States (as well as the Common Market for Eastern and Southern Africa and the Southern African Development Community), but has taken limited advantage of this access so far.

In addition to targeting the production of apparel (see below), Zambia could consider spinning and exporting yarn and fabric, intermediate steps between cotton production and apparel. A recent study identified Zambia as one of the most feasible locations in Sub-Saharan Africa for an export-oriented cotton spinning mill (UNIDO 2011). The already well-established cotton industry, which produces high-quality cotton (Zambian cotton commands a premium on world markets), and the expansion potential of cheap hydroelectricity may facilitate this step. If feasible, such a strategy could foster backward links and help Zambia capture more value from its raw materials.[4] To this end, Zambia should actively seek foreign direct investment to make up for the shortage in domestic financing and skilled manpower. In the absence of a competitive apparel sector, the majority of yarn and fabric output may initially have to be exported, perhaps to other African countries with more competitive apparel industries and eligible for preferential access to U.S. markets under the African Growth and Opportunity Act preferences.[5] Because high input costs are a major constraint on the competitiveness of the apparel sector (see below), filling in this missing link in the supply chain might contribute to the development of a more competitive sector in the long run.

The Main Constraints on Competitiveness

Taking polo shirts as an indicator of production costs in the wider apparel sector, we find that the costs of producing apparel are higher in Zambia than in China (approximately $4.60 per shirt compared with $4.07). There are several reasons for the difference in production costs between well-managed firms in the two countries (figure 5.2). Zambia has a labor cost advantage because wages in Zambia are about 50 percent less than wages in China. This would represent a 5 percent overall cost advantage except that the advantage is nearly canceled out by the lower labor efficiency in Zambia.[6] Ultimately, the higher trade logistics and input costs and the slightly higher overhead and financing costs in Zambia raise the total cost per polo shirt 13 percent above the corresponding cost in China.

The three main constraints on Zambia's competitiveness in apparel are poor trade logistics, low labor efficiency, and high input costs.

Poor Trade Logistics

Zambia suffers from poor trade logistics, a particular disadvantage among large firms (which are more likely to export), although all firms are affected to some extent because of the need to import inputs.[7] Because Zambia is landlocked, many inputs and all outputs exported outside the region must be transported through the ports at Dar es Salaam or Durban, which are more than 1,900 and 2,100 kilometers from Lusaka, respectively.

Figure 5.2 The Cost to Produce a Polo Shirt, Zambia Relative to China

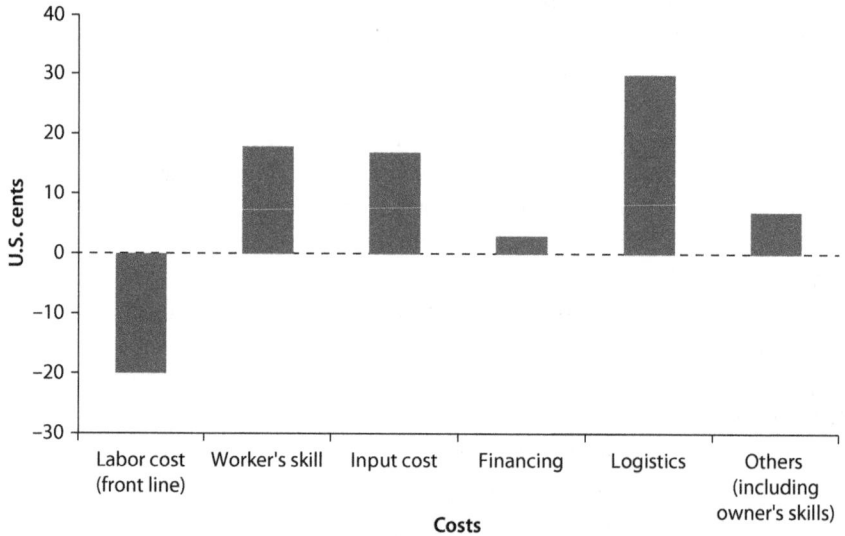

Sources: World Bank based on a value chain analysis of polo shirts in China by Global Development Solutions (GDS 2011).
Note: For Zambia, rough estimates are derived from a value chain analysis for men's underwear and five in-depth interviews conducted among apparel companies by the World Bank in July 2009.

A low ranking on the trading-across-borders component of the World Bank's doing business index illustrates the challenges Zambia faces.[8] Despite ranking 84 among 153 countries on the overall doing business index, Zambia ranks 153 among 183 countries on trading across borders, including a relatively significant amount of time required to export and a high cost to import or export goods. Compared with China, the cost to import or export is substantial in Zambia. It costs $3,315 to import a 20-foot, 10-ton container to Zambia compared with $545 to China, and $2,678 to export a container from Zambia compared with $500 from China. More than 85 percent of the cost difference derives from the higher inland transportation and handling costs in Zambia (around 20 times greater than in China).

Similarly, the time to export or import a container is more than two times greater in Zambia than in China. Half the difference arises because of the extra time for document preparation, and one-third because of the extra time for inland transportation, including delays at intermediate borders and because of poor-quality roads.[9] On the north-south corridor that connects Zambia with the ports of Dar es Salaam and Durban, journey times are typically one-third driving and two-thirds waiting (TMSA 2011). Delays at the Beitbridge (Zimbabwe) and Chirundu (Zambia) border posts result in an estimated 25 percent surcharge on transport costs along the corridor (Teravaninthorn and Raballand 2009).[10] Some of the disadvantage is offset by Zambia's relatively competitive trucking industry, which charges lower costs per ton-kilometer than the trucking industries in other African countries (Raballand and Whitworth 2011).

Low Worker Skill

Labor efficiency in Zambia is low because of lower worker skills and motivation, outdated equipment (resulting from a long period of industrial decline and lack of investment), small-scale operations, and captive customers, allowing firms to survive well below optimal productivity levels. Interviews conducted for this study identified a major concern among managers at apparel firms because labor laws and regulations are adversely affecting labor costs and worker motivation by making it difficult to compensate based on performance (for example, piece rates), to lay off workers (for instance, for theft), to hire skilled foreign workers to train Zambian workers, and to employ women (who are entitled to generous, but unfunded, maternity benefits). Wages in the informal sector—where workers and firms are not subject to the same regulations—are much lower, and motivation and productivity are reportedly higher.

Aside from the impact on productivity and, thus, on overall labor costs, many of these factors also contribute to low product quality; for example, employers have few tools to encourage workers to put in extra effort to produce export-quality products. And because of the cushion provided by contracts with captive customers, firms have limited incentives to improve service or quality.

High Input Costs: The Absence of Competitive Input Industries

In the polo shirt example, raw materials such as fabric, collars, thread, and buttons account for more than 70 percent of the production costs. Zambia produces high-quality cotton, a major input for polo shirts, but the local production of cotton does not translate into lower input costs for Zambian textile and apparel producers. The domestic price of cotton is high; the spinning and textiles industries are weak; and all Zambia's cotton is exported as lint.

There are substantial inefficiencies in the cotton-to-apparel value chain, and Zambian apparel producers are forced to import most of their inputs from Asia at high cost.[11] A quantitative survey of small and medium firms in the five countries that are the focus of this study found that African firms are more likely to rely on imported inputs than Asian firms of equivalent size. Few manufacturers import inputs directly, however; sample firms imported most of their inputs through local traders (World Bank 2011a). Poor trade logistics thus reinforce the disadvantage of high input costs.

The key vertically integrated textile mills were Kafue Textiles and Zambia-China Mulungushi Textiles Joint Venture Ltd., a joint collaboration of the Zambian government (34 percent) and the Chinese government (66 percent) in 1997. The latter was the largest textile company in Zambia, employing 2,000 workers and producing 100,000 garments a year. Over time, the company set up its own cotton ginneries, but it then failed in 2008 because of high production costs, inadequate funds to run and upgrade the mill's obsolete equipment, and the inability to take advantage of favorable policies. To resuscitate the industry, the government has recently revived the Mulungushi Textile Mill as a joint venture and is installing new machines and state-of-the-art technology to make the company competitive.

Light Manufacturing in Zambia • http://dx.doi.org/10.1596/978-0-8213-9935-4

Because of the high production costs, most of the large garment enterprises have closed or are for sale, including Swarp Spinning Mills. As of 2010, there were only eight garment enterprises left in the country. The Zambian textile and garment industry is now struggling to survive. Imports of secondhand clothes have contributed to the industry's decline. Most of the surviving companies now spin yarn from locally grown cotton for export, while others are producing woven and knitted fabrics for the domestic market, but at far below capacity.

Recommendations

Overall, the case of the textile and garment industry in Zambia demonstrates the delicate balance required between the state and the market. Past policy interventions in the market (such as those in the 1970s and 1980s) led to disastrous economic consequences. But complete reliance on the market (such as in the 1990s) left the private sector to struggle with issues beyond its capabilities and control and did not solve Zambia's growth and diversification problem.

To help create productive employment, the government has to work closely with the private sector to remove the bottlenecks in light manufacturing. Following liberalization in the early 1990s, the role of the government in the economy has been curtailed, but a true partnership has never been established. To move the dynamic informal sector into the formal sector, it is essential that the government act as and be perceived to be a stakeholder in private sector development.

The strategy for Zambia to grow the textiles and apparel sector should address the problem of imports of secondhand clothing and issues related to production costs.

The government's failure to control the imports of donated secondhand garments has proved disastrous for the Zambian garment industry. Secondhand garments from the West flooded the Zambian market.[12] This market grew a remarkable 600 percent over 15 years, as charitable clothing donations (Goodwill Industries, Oxfam, the Salvation Army) were sold by for-profit brokers, exporters, and used clothing resellers, all of whom charged a markup. Although the quality of locally made clothes is better, consumers opt for the cheaper imported products. Instead of relying only on market forces, the Zambian government could have petitioned the World Trade Organization or introduced safeguard legislation to allow temporary duties to be levied on the imports that were flooding the market.

The competitiveness of Zambia's textiles and apparel sector could be enhanced over time by reducing production costs and boosting productivity. To this end, the recommended priority actions are as follows:

- *Improve trade logistics:* Import-export cost and time comparisons suggest that there are two important means of improving trade logistics among Zambian apparel manufacturers: reducing the time required to prepare import-export documents (particularly letters of credit, which account for over a quarter of the time required to import or export a container) and reducing the waiting time at borders (waiting time accounts for two-thirds of journey times on the north-south corridor).[13]

One-stop border posts could greatly reduce the waiting time at borders. Such posts share physical facilities (a common control zone with a fenced perimeter and common facilities, including scanning, weighbridges, and inspection bays), operations, and training and a common legal framework (TMSA 2011). A one-stop border post was recently established at Chirundu, between Zambia and Zimbabwe, and has reportedly cut the time to cross the border by more than half (from four or five days to two days or even only a few hours), thus lowering transportation costs (TMSA 2011). Efforts are also under way to improve the efficiency of other border posts affecting Zambian importers and exporters (for example, the border between Zambia and Tanzania), but this will require strong regional cooperation and coordination among multiple agencies in each country. Regional cooperation is even more critical for improving the efficiency of the border crossings that affect Zambia's trade, but that are not under Zambia's control, such as the intermediate border crossings between Botswana, South Africa, and Zimbabwe.

- *Provide workers and managers with the training, incentives, and equipment necessary to improve productivity and product quality:* Engaging foreign investors in initiatives to upgrade technology and providing technical assistance to train local workers and managers could help Zambian apparel firms boost their productivity and the quality of their products. Chinese firms are much more likely than Zambian and other African firms to rely on external experts at start-up and, subsequently, when introducing new products, changing technology or modifying distribution systems, thereby conferring a strong advantage (World Bank 2011a). Kaizen training is one instrument that could be used.[14] Higher productivity and quality could also be encouraged by increasing the flexibility of labor markets, particularly by making the introduction of performance-based compensation components easier so as to strengthen worker incentives.

- *Facilitate the development of competitive input industries such as spinning and textiles:* Like Ethiopia, Zambia may be able to fill a major gap in the cotton-to-apparel value chain by developing a more competitive spinning and textile industry. Zambia's favorable conditions for cotton production and its hydro-electric potential could facilitate this. A detailed feasibility study could determine if this is warranted. A competitive domestic supply of cotton fabric could reduce production costs and delivery delays in the apparel sector by lessening the reliance on imported inputs. Facilitating partnerships between ginners and cotton farmers could support farmers in planting, growing, and harvesting cotton; 90 percent of cotton is grown on small-scale farms, where there is room to improve productivity. To deal with the cartel of ginneries selling domestic cotton at Liverpool prices, the government should follow the example of Kenya and Lesotho by facilitating competition among cotton sellers so as to prevent a single private cotton seller from charging the export-parity price to local textile manufacturers, thereby lowering production costs for spinners, textile manufacturers, and apparel producers.

- *Establish a plug-and-play industrial park:* Several constraints could be eased simultaneously if a plug-and-play industrial park were available. China has shown that such parks can assist firms by providing affordable access to industrial land, standardized factory shell buildings, and worker housing, as well as training facilities and one-stop shops for complying with business regulations. Industrial parks lower the financing costs and risks for well-performing small firms, allowing them to grow larger even if banks consider them too risky for loans.

- *Establish a partnership between government and the private sector to address the key constraints in the sector:* This would include dealing with secondhand clothing through a petition to the World Trade Organization or introducing safeguard legislation, or both.

Notes

1. In contrast, in Ethiopia, the sector employed 9,000 workers and exported $8 million worth of apparel in 2009, while, in Vietnam, the sector employed 1 million workers and exported $8 billion worth of apparel.
2. Zambia's textile sector produces primarily 100 percent cotton yarn, along with small quantities of blended yarn. Most of the yarn is exported, but a small share is retained for the domestic production of woven fabric used to manufacture niche apparel articles (USITC 2009).
3. Producers of cotton products claim that a cartel of ginneries refuses to sell cotton on the domestic market at less than the Liverpool price, some 25 percent higher than the price should be without transport costs. At this price, they claim, Zambian cotton is twice as costly as cotton in China.
4. This would need to be considered carefully given the spinning industry's collapse in Zambia in recent years. For example, Swarp, Zambia's largest textile mill and one of Sub-Saharan Africa's leading producers and exporters of 100 percent cotton yarns and blended cotton-polyester yarns, collapsed in 2008, in part because of labor management problems. Swarp sourced most of its cotton lint domestically and, at its peak, employed more than 1,000 workers. Having become internationally competitive in the production and export of cotton yarn, Swarp was seen as a Zambian success story (USITC 2009).
5. For example, even after Zambia became eligible under the African Growth and Opportunity Act in 2004, Swarp exported cotton yarn to Botswana, Mauritius, and South Africa to be used in products eligible under the act rather than exporting directly to the United States.
6. Wage rates are higher in Zambia than in other African economies and Vietnam. However, because of severe competitive pressure, apparel workers in Zambia are not

highly paid by local standards. Nonetheless, relative to Ethiopia, formal sector workers in the apparel industry in Zambia are paid 50 percent more for skilled labor and 200 percent more for unskilled labor.

7. The World Bank (2011a) finds that small and medium enterprises in light manufacturing in Africa, especially in landlocked countries such as Zambia, are much less likely to export than firms in China (and, to a lesser extent, Vietnam). In 2010, almost 80 percent of Zambian manufacturing firms imported some or all of their inputs, and over one-quarter imported 100 percent of their inputs (ZAM 2011).

8. This section draws on data in Doing Business (database), International Finance Corporation and World Bank, Washington, DC, http://www.doingbusiness.org/data.

9. The time required for inland transportation is estimated separately from the cost, but the cost implicitly includes the cost of delays because the trucking companies set prices based partly on the time spent waiting at borders.

10. Import duties are a less significant issue because tax incentives allow eligible firms to import textile machinery, all woven polyester fabric for processing, and all sewing threads and gray fabric duty-free (ZRA 2007).

11. For example, four of the estimated eight firms in the textile sector are vertically integrated, spinning their own yarn for use in finished textile and apparel production (USITC 2009).

12. While many goods are donated by charities, the market is dominated by small traders who make millions of dollars in aggregate by selling these clothes for less than a dollar each. The used clothing shipped to Sub-Saharan Africa by the United States accounts for nearly $60 million in sales annually. Wholesalers mark prices up by as much as 400 percent.

13. According to information provided by the World Bank's doing business team, it takes 14 days to obtain a letter of credit in Zambia. See Doing Business (database), International Finance Corporation and World Bank, Washington, DC, http://www .doingbusiness.org/data.

14. Kaizen training conducted as part of this study had a significant impact on production management, recordkeeping, and business performance in Tanzania's garment industry (World Bank 2011a). Training programs for Zambia should take into account that training workers might take longer there than in countries such as China and Ethiopia. In China and Ethiopia, 85–90 percent of firms covered by our survey reported that it takes at most four weeks for new workers to be fully trained, whereas, in Tanzania and Zambia, less than 60 percent of firms reported that new workers are trained in four weeks or less (World Bank 2011b).

References

Chikoti, S., and C. Q. Mutonga. 2002. "Textiles and Clothing in Zambia." Report, Ministry of Commerce, Trade, and Industry, Lusaka.

GDS (Global Development Solutions). 2011. *The Value Chain and Feasibility Analysis; Domestic Resource Cost Analysis.* Vol. 2 of *Light Manufacturing in Africa: Targeted Policies to Enhance Private Investment and Create Jobs.* Washington, DC: World Bank. http://go.worldbank.org/6G2A3TFI20.

Raballand, Gaël, and Alan Whitworth. 2011. "Should the Zambian Government Invest in Railways?" ZIPAR Working Paper 3, Zambia Institute for Policy Analysis and Research, Lusaka.

Teravaninthorn, Supee, and Gaël Raballand. 2009. *Transport Prices and Costs in Africa: A Review of the International Corridors.* Directions in Development Series: Infrastructure. Washington, DC: World Bank.

TMSA (TradeMark Southern Africa). 2011. "Case Study: Chirundu One Stop Border Post." TMSA Case Study Series, TMSA, Pretoria. http://www.trademarksa.org/publications/tmsa-case-study-series-chirundu-one-stop-border-post.

UNIDO (United Nations Industrial Development Organization). 2011. *Feasibility Study for a Cotton Spinning Mill in 11 Sub-Saharan African Countries.* Vienna.

USITC (United States International Trade Commission). 2009. "Sub-Saharan African Textile and Apparel Inputs: Potential for Competitive Production." Investigation 332–502, USITC Publication 4078, Washington, DC: USITC.

World Bank. 2011a. *Kaizen for Managerial Skills Improvement in Small and Medium Enterprises: An Impact Evaluation Study.* Vol. 4 of *Light Manufacturing in Africa: Targeted Policies to Enhance Private Investment and Create Jobs.* Washington, DC: World Bank. http://go.worldbank.org/4Y1QF5FIB0.

———. 2011b. *Background Papers.* Vol. 3 of *Light Manufacturing in Africa: Targeted Policies to Enhance Private Investment and Create Jobs.* Washington, DC: World Bank. http://go.worldbank.org/LIX5E1FI90.

ZAM (Zambia Association of Manufacturers). 2011. "Zambia Manufacturing Industry Sector Audit, 2011." ZAM, Lusaka.

ZRA (Zambia Revenue Authority). 2007. "Tax Incentives." Lusaka. http://www.zra.org.zm/Tax_Incentives.php.

CHAPTER 6

Leather Products

Introduction

The strong potential for expanding the livestock industry and the low capacity utilization at tanneries point to the possibility for Zambia to produce and export more leather and leather products. Supporting ongoing efforts to expand livestock herds and facilitating improvements in the quality of hides could enable Zambia to exploit more of its potential in leather. Easing some key constraints might make it feasible to produce more leather products as well.

Zambia's leather industry is small and oriented primarily toward producing leather rather than higher–value added leather products. In 2010, Zambia exported $2.3 million worth of leather products; Vietnam exported a thousand times that amount.[1] Of the total hides collected, about 80 percent are processed into wet blue before export (Simpelwe 2011).

Six of the eight firms operating in the leather products sector produce leather footwear.[2] Employment is estimated at 600 people (around 2,000 if informal microenterprises are included).[3] The domestic production of leather products is limited to industrial safety boots (many are also imported), military boots, school shoes, sandals, and a few other products such as handbags, belts, and footballs. Leather fashion shoes and casual shoes are not produced in Zambia.

The market and the institutional support structure for footwear in Zambia is outlined in figure 6.1. The input part of the supply chain is weak, and many inputs are imported. Furthermore, the sector faces competition from imported new and secondhand footwear.

Sectoral Potential

Zambia has the potential to increase the supply of leather products to domestic and regional markets, as well as to export wet blue and finished leather. The sector benefits from some advantages that could support greater competitiveness over time, as follows:

- *A substantial labor cost advantage over China:* The advantage is greater in shoes than in apparel because the leather sector is more labor intensive; labor

Figure 6.1 The Footwear Market and Institutional Support Structure, Zambia

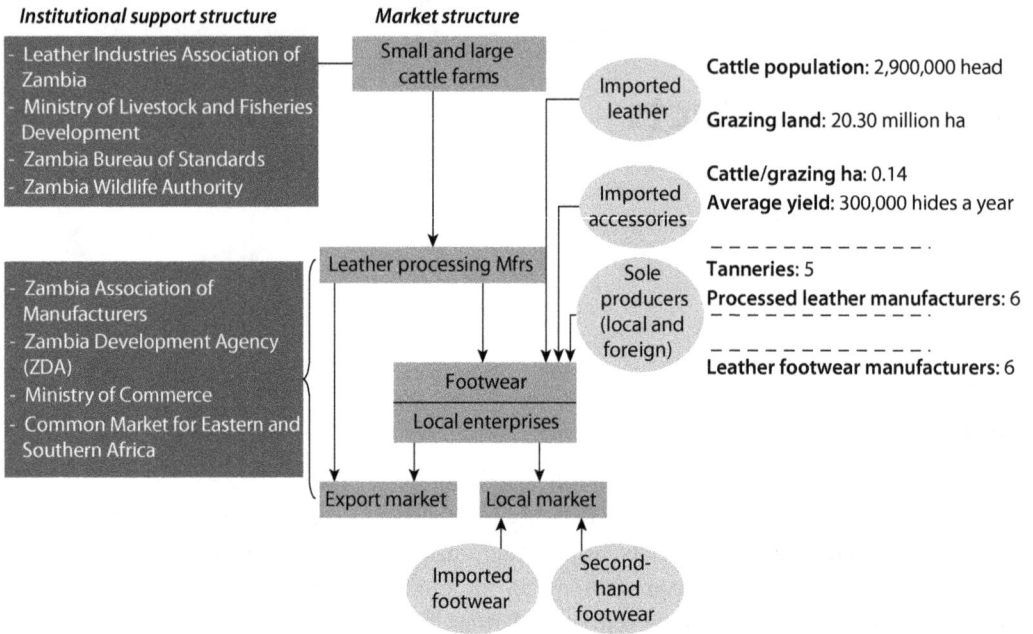

Institutional support structure   *Market structure*

- Leather Industries Association of Zambia
- Ministry of Livestock and Fisheries Development
- Zambia Bureau of Standards
- Zambia Wildlife Authority

Small and large cattle farms

Imported leather

Cattle population: 2,900,000 head

Grazing land: 20.30 million ha

Imported accessories

Cattle/grazing ha: 0.14
Average yield: 300,000 hides a year

- Zambia Association of Manufacturers
- Zambia Development Agency (ZDA)
- Ministry of Commerce
- Common Market for Eastern and Southern Africa

Leather processing Mfrs

Sole producers (local and foreign)

Tanneries: 5
Processed leather manufacturers: 6

Leather footwear manufacturers: 6

Footwear

Local enterprises

Export market   Local market

Imported footwear   Second-hand footwear

Source: GDS 2011.
Note: Dashed lines indicate a weak link, lack of organization, and areas where technical support is required to strengthen ties along the supply chain.

accounts for 40 percent of the production cost of leather shoes in China, compared with 10 percent in the case of apparel. Zambia combines low wages with good labor efficiency that is on a par with labor efficiency in China (figure 6.2).

- *Potential to expand the cattle industry greatly by more fully exploiting Zambia's extensive grazing land (currently exhibiting low cattle density) to meet the rising domestic and regional demand for beef and dairy products:* The leather industry—a largely undervalued and underexploited by-product of the beef and dairy industries—could be expanded in conjunction with these industries. Zambia's carrying capacity suggests that the country could support more than 7 million cattle, more than twice the current 3 million (World Bank 2011a).

- *Opportunities for increasing the numbers of skins of other animals, particularly in the burgeoning crocodile skin industry:* The number of crocodile skins exported by Zambia doubled between 2002 and 2009, albeit with some annual fluctuations (Caldwell 2011).

- *Duty-free access of leather products:* Zambian leather products enjoy duty-free access to markets in the European Union and the United States and preferential access to the markets of members of the Common Market for Eastern and Southern Africa and the Southern African Development Community.

Figure 6.2 The Cost to Produce Leather Shoes, Zambia Relative to China

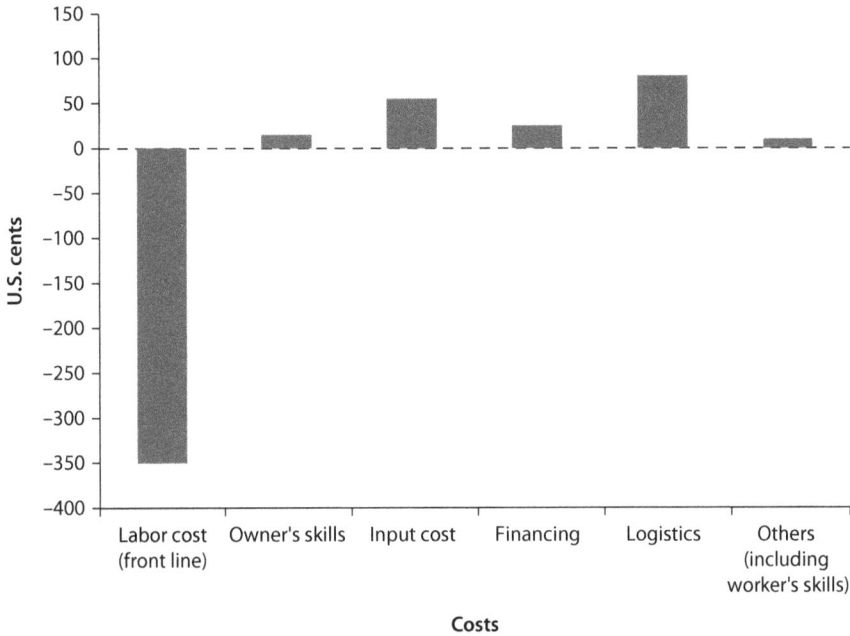

Source: World Bank, based on a value chain analysis for leather loafers in China by Global Development Solutions (GDS 2011) and rough estimates derived from in-depth company interviews conducted by the World Bank in July 2009.

The Main Constraints on Competitiveness

The cost of producing and exporting leather shoes to the European Union and the United States is lower for Zambia than for China (figure 6.2). Zambia's considerable labor cost advantage, though smaller than Ethiopia's, for example, outweighs disadvantages in other factors.

However, Zambia's leather shoe production is less competitive with China than it could be because of poor trade logistics and high input costs. Furthermore, while production costs are lower in Zambia than in China, they are higher in Zambia than in Ethiopia, Tanzania, and Vietnam (table 6.1). This is largely the result of higher labor costs in Zambia relative to Ethiopia and, to a lesser extent, Vietnam and worse trade logistics relative to Vietnam. These issues are discussed in more detail below.

The main issues in the leather products sector concern inputs, trade logistics, worker skills, and technology.

Shortage of Inputs

A lack of the domestic production of several key inputs, including leather and chemicals, means that these inputs have to be imported. The shortage of high-quality raw hides and skins lowers capacity utilization at tanneries (50–65 percent). Tanneries face the choice of importing hides and skins, wet blue, and finished leather or using poor-quality raw materials to produce

Table 6.1 Production Cost Advantage or Disadvantage in Leather Loafers, Four Countries Relative to China
US$ per pair of shoes

Indicator	China	Advantage or disadvantage relative to China			
		Ethiopia	*Tanzania*	*Zambia*[a]	*Vietnam*
Labor cost	6.50	−5.50	−3.50	−3.50	−4.10
Labor efficiency		+0.20	0	0	+1.00
Capital cost	0.15	+0.5	+0.10 (land)[a]	+0.5	0
Capital efficiency		+0.5	+0.15	+0.10	+0.50
Input cost	7.00	+0.35 (with imported leather)	+0.20	+0.20	+0.15
Input efficiency		+0.70	+0.35	+0.35	−0.35
Utility cost and usage	0.10	0	+0.10	0	+0.50
Financing cost	0.35	+0.25	+0.25	+0.25	0
Trade logistics cost (European Union, United States)	0.55	+0.70	n.a. (no exports)	+0.80	0
Overhead and regulatory cost	0.15	+0.10 (rough estimate)	+0.35 (low volume)	+0.10	+0.20
Total production cost	14.80	11.70	12.80	13.15	11.80

Source: World Bank, based on a value chain analysis by Global Development Solutions of leather loafers in China, Ethiopia, and Tanzania and on rough estimates derived from interviews among companies in Zambia in July 2009.
Note: + = a disadvantage relative to China; − = an advantage relative to China; n.a. = not applicable.
a. Rough estimates.

poor-quality products. Several factors contribute to the shortage of high-quality hides and skins:

- *The supply chain is weak:* Most of the cattle farming sector operates on a nonintegrated basis across the meat, milk, and hides segments.
- *Many hides are exported:* Despite a ban on exporting raw hides, there is a brisk illegal trade in hides by traders seeking better prices. The majority of hides are exported as wet blue rather than processed (encouraged by the fact that wet blue exports to China are duty-free).
- *Farmers fail to appreciate the potential value of the hides and skins:* When combined with a lack of knowledge and training, this leads to poor branding, slaughter, and preservation techniques that damage hides and skins. Of the 70 percent of hides that originate in the traditional sector, almost 30 percent are rejected for inferior quality. Hides produced in the commercial sector are usually of good quality.
- *Poor livestock management:* Poor management leads to damage to hides from ticks and other pests and diseases.

Trade Logistics

The production cost of a cowhide shoe made in Zambia is twice that of a sheepskin loafer made in Ethiopia and nearly as expensive as a loafer made in China, largely because of the high cost of the imported materials associated with lasting and finishing. High transport and trade logistics costs and high import tariffs on some inputs—for instance, 25 percent on finished leather and 15–25 percent on midsoles and outsoles—all contribute to the high cost of imported materials. There have been some improvements in trade policy in the past decade that have reduced some costs. The import duty on the PVC (polyvinyl chloride) lining and eyelets used in shoe production was reduced to 5 percent, and the duty on tannery machinery and equipment was removed in 2001. Exporters benefit from a duty drawback scheme, but firms supplying the domestic market do not receive rebates on import duties (ZRA 2007) (for more details on transport and trade logistics costs, see chapter 5 on apparel).

Labor Cost, Efficiency, and Skills

Zambian manufacturers of leather shoes compare favorably with their counterparts in China and Vietnam. Labor costs are lower in Zambia than in China, and labor efficiency is comparable, while the higher labor efficiency in Zambia relative to Vietnam outweighs the positive effect of Vietnam's lower wages. Another concern is inadequate labor skills. Two Zambia-based leather product firms claimed to have raised productivity as much as 50 percent by investing in worker training in India and in special training programs in Zambia.

Technology

Outdated technology is an additional constraint on the competitiveness of Zambia's leather products sector. In particular, obsolete machinery and the lack of design expertise limit production to simple, lower-quality, or niche products that cannot compete on the international market.

Recommendations

Several actions could improve Zambia's competitiveness in leather products:[4]

- *Remove the export ban on unprocessed leather:* Removing the ban could increase the returns to cattle farmers, encourage investment in this critical part of the leather products supply chain, and ultimately raise the supply of hides.

- *Attract foreign investors:* Particularly in tanning, more foreign investment could boost productivity and quality and strengthen the links between Zambia's leather products sector and the international market. More than in some other light manufacturing sectors (such as wood products and apparel), foreign investors seem interested in Zambia's leather sector. For example, in 2009, TATA spent $1.2 million to take over an insolvent tannery in Zambia. More recently, a group of Indian investors expressed interest in partnering with leather producers in the Common Market for Eastern and Southern Africa to establish a regional leather industry, including supporting improved technologies and importing leather worth $1.5 billion from Zambia over the next five years (Muganya 2011).

- *Facilitate knowledge sharing:* Zambia's leather products sector could benefit from better management and design skills, especially if these are facilitated by external experts. Kaizen training and foreign investors could play important roles. The survey of small and medium firms conducted for this study found that Chinese firms are much more likely than African firms to rely on external experts at start-up and at subsequent stages (the introduction of new products, changes in technology, modifications in distribution systems) (World Bank 2011b; see also chapter 5). In addition to standard managerial and technical training, Zambia's leather goods sector could benefit from foreign involvement in training in up-to-date design skills, which would allow firms to manufacture more fashionable products that would appeal to higher-end and international markets. Another way to foster the skills needed to manufacture leather shoes competitively for domestic and regional markets is through collaboration among developing countries in trade schools and small and medium producers of simple leather products, such as handbags and school bags, that would encourage Zambians to produce these goods.[5] Zambian firms should also seek to learn from their regional peers—for example, through initiatives of the Common Market for Eastern and Southern Africa—to share lessons related to the leather sector.

- *Encourage backward and forward links along the value chain:* Initiatives that foster tighter links between raw material suppliers and end producers would benefit poor indigenous farmers, as well as major firms, which stand to gain from a better supply of higher-quality leather (and beef and milk).[6] The experience of a few vertically integrated companies has shown that Zambia can produce leather of the highest quality (for example, the exports for Jaguar cars).

- *Improve trade logistics:* Better trade logistics would reduce production costs and the time to receive inputs and ship the final product to the customer. Efforts to improve trade logistics should be undertaken in collaboration with neighboring countries (see the discussion in chapter 5).

Over the longer term, Zambia can increase the availability of high-quality leather by promoting the development of the livestock industry. Targeted actions can be taken to encourage the leather, beef, and dairy industries to develop hand in hand. The following efforts, many of which have already been initiated and aimed at expanding the beef and dairy industries, will also benefit the leather products sector by increasing the quantity and quality of hides:

- *Improve disease control:* The skin diseases impairing leather quality can be reduced through a vaccination program to reduce the incidence of ectoparasites. In Ethiopia, the cost for such a vaccination program was less than $10 million for the entire country (Dinh and others 2012). This would make a major contribution to the number and quality of hides.

- *Improve breeding and feeding practices:* Better breeding and feeding practices would increase cattle numbers and raise the quality of the hides.

- *Educate traditional farmers:* The traditional sector raises 80 percent of the country's cattle. Educating traditional farmers and improving their animal husbandry skills and market awareness could greatly increase cattle numbers, productivity, and hide quality and help integrate the farmers into the formal supply chain. One successful effort has been the establishment by the Leather Industry Association of Zambia and the Zambia Bureau of Standards of a standards and grading system for raw hides and skins for use by abattoirs, traders, and tanneries. The system has improved supplier awareness of the quality standards for hides and reduced hide rejection rates at leather factories.

For a more detailed discussion of how the competitiveness of the beef and dairy industries could be improved, see World Bank (2011a). Similar actions could be taken for other types of livestock.

Notes

1. UN Comtrade (United Nations Commodity Trade Statistics Database), Statistics Division, Department of Economic and Social Affairs, United Nations, New York, http://comtrade.un.org/db.
2. At the time of research, one of the leather footwear firms was performing poorly and was considered likely to go out of business soon.
3. Data are based on information gathered by Global Development Solutions (GDS 2011). This compares with 7,600 in Ethiopia, 1,000 in Tanzania, and more than 600,000 in Vietnam.
4. The leather products sector in Zambia has a considerable labor cost advantage over the sector in China; so, reducing wages is not included here as a priority.
5. In all of low-income South Asia, the domestic availability of leather and trade schools has fostered the development of an indigenous slippers and sandals industry that has evolved into a shoe industry.
6. An example is TATA Zambia's 2009 memorandum of understanding with the government, whereby TATA would train small-scale farmers and personnel at abattoirs on the production of quality hides and the treatment of hides before they are supplied to TATA's tannery (ZDA 2009).

References

Caldwell, John. 2011. "World Trade in Crocodilian Skins 2007–2009." International Alligator and Crocodile Trade Study, World Conservation Monitoring Center, United Nations Environment Programme, Cambridge.

Dinh, Hinh T., Vincent Palmade, Vandana Chandra, and Frances Cossar. 2012. *Light Manufacturing in Africa: Targeted Policies to Enhance Private Investment and Create Jobs.* Washington, DC: World Bank. https://openknowledge.worldbank.org/handle/10986/2245.

GDS (Global Development Solutions). 2011. *The Value Chain and Feasibility Analysis; Domestic Resource Cost Analysis.* Vol. 2 of *Light Manufacturing in Africa: Targeted Policies to Enhance Private Investment and Create Jobs.* Washington, DC: World Bank. http://go.worldbank.org/6G2A3TFI20.

Muganya, Nchimunya. 2011. "Promoting Leather Industry Critical to Nation's Economic Development." *Times of Zambia,* Ndola, Zambia. http://allafrica.com/stories/201105040378.html.

Simpelwe, Ndinawe. 2011. "Minister Calls for Value Addition in Leather Sector." *Post Online,* Post Newspapers, Lusaka. http://www.postzambia.com/post-read_article.php?articleId=20209.

World Bank. 2011a. "Zambia: What Would It Take for Zambia's Beef and Dairy Industries to Achieve Their Potential?" Report 62377-ZM, Finance and Private Sector Development Unit, Africa Region, World Bank, Washington, DC.

———. 2011b. *Background Papers.* Vol. 3 of *Light Manufacturing in Africa: Targeted Policies to Enhance Private Investment and Create Jobs.* Washington, DC: World Bank. http://go.worldbank.org/LIX5E1FI90.

ZDA (Zambia Development Agency). 2009. "ZDA and TATA Sign MoU." *ZDA Spotlight* 3, ZDA, Lusaka.

ZRA (Zambia Revenue Authority). 2007. "Tax Incentives." ZRA, Lusaka. http://www.zra.org.zm/Tax_Incentives.php.

CHAPTER 7

Wood Products

Introduction

The main opportunity for Zambia's wood products sector is in the domestic market. Greater international competitiveness might be achievable over the longer term through improvements in the availability of upgraded technology and skills, support for more efficient supply chains, and access to reasonably priced domestic wood.

Zambia exports mostly raw wood and reimports processed wood from China and South Africa, such as standardized low-cost furniture. In 2009, Zambia imported wood and wood products worth approximately $20.8 million and exported goods worth about $7.8 million, resulting in a negative trade balance in processed wood products. By 2010, following a rapid decline in the exports of wooden furniture, imports valued at $6.2 million outweighed exports by a factor of more than 400.[1]

Zambia produces value added wood products made of softwood and hardwood. The domestic market, mainly the construction industry, consumes 70 percent of the processed wood products including sawn wood, and the rest is exported, nearly all to the Democratic Republic of Congo.

The wood products sector employs more than 47,000 people, mostly men. There are an estimated 600 formal sector firms and more than 3,000 generally small informal sector firms. Although more than 96 percent of the registered wood processing companies are categorized as small and medium enterprises, less than 10 percent of all exported wood products are produced by small and medium enterprises, which are usually low-productivity, informal sector firms producing low-quality products. There are a few formal sector firms that export high-value products (such as hardwood floors) and that have started to compete with imports of simpler products, such as window frames and doors. Foreign investment in furniture has been minimal and does not seem to be increasing. Figure 7.1 shows the supply chain and institutional structure in wood products in Zambia.

Figure 7.1 The Processed Wood Supply Chain and Institutional Support Structure, Zambia

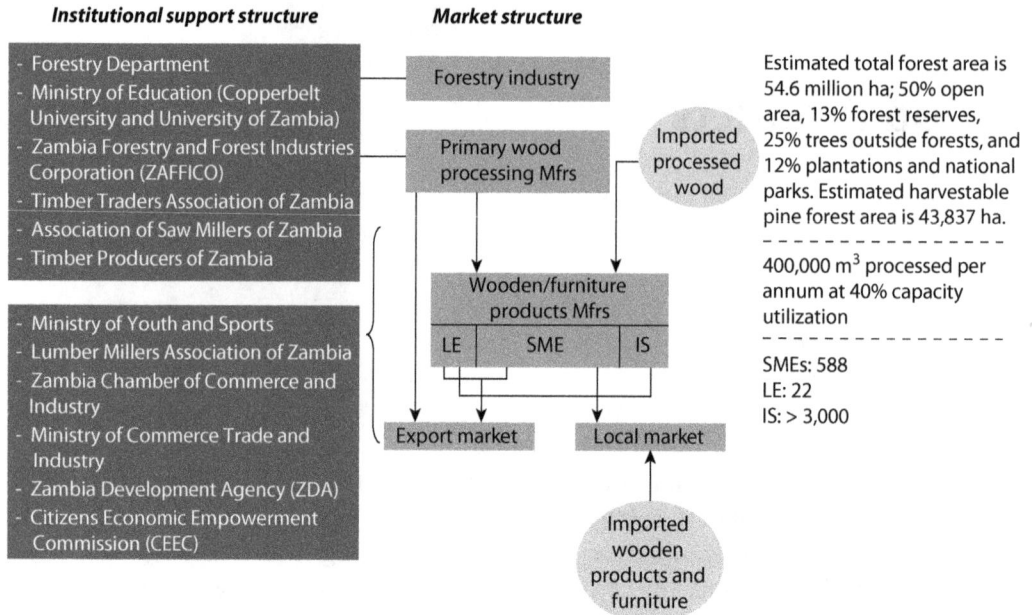

Institutional support structure   *Market structure*

- Forestry Department
- Ministry of Education (Copperbelt University and University of Zambia)
- Zambia Forestry and Forest Industries Corporation (ZAFFICO)
- Timber Traders Association of Zambia
- Association of Saw Millers of Zambia
- Timber Producers of Zambia

- Ministry of Youth and Sports
- Lumber Millers Association of Zambia
- Zambia Chamber of Commerce and Industry
- Ministry of Commerce Trade and Industry
- Zambia Development Agency (ZDA)
- Citizens Economic Empowerment Commission (CEEC)

Forestry industry

Primary wood processing Mfrs

Imported processed wood

Wooden/furniture products Mfrs

| LE | SME | IS |

Export market   Local market

Imported wooden products and furniture

Estimated total forest area is 54.6 million ha; 50% open area, 13% forest reserves, 25% trees outside forests, and 12% plantations and national parks. Estimated harvestable pine forest area is 43,837 ha.
- - - - - - - - - - - - - - -
400,000 m^3 processed per annum at 40% capacity utilization
- - - - - - - - - - - - - - -
SMEs: 588
LE: 22
IS: > 3,000

Source: GDS 2011.
Note: Dashed lines indicate a weak link, lack of organization, and areas where technical support is required to strengthen ties along the supply chain; LE = large enterprise; SME = small and medium enterprise; IS = informal sector.

Sectoral Potential

Zambia has a comparative advantage in growing trees for wood: the country's forests, which cover 54.6 million hectares, include high-value wood trees such as teak, mahogany, rosewood, and pine. Yet, based on the domestic resource cost ratio for wooden chairs, Zambia's global competitive position in wood products is weak (GDS 2011). It will take time to achieve the productivity increases required to become internationally competitive. Over the medium term, the sector is expected to focus primarily on the rapidly growing domestic market to support the construction industry and to meet the demand for products that are currently being imported, but that are nonetheless relatively simple to make.

The Main Constraints on Competitiveness

Taking wooden chairs as illustrative of the manufacturing of wood products more generally, we find that Zambia is not internationally competitive in the sector. A wooden chair that on average costs $12.67 to make in China and $17.50 in Vietnam costs $30.97 in the formal sector in Zambia However, the cost of production in Zambia is competitive in the region: a similar chair costs $40.38 to produce in Ethiopia and $31.21 in Tanzania.

While the cost of wooden chairs produced in Zambia's informal sector is well below the $30.97 cost in the formal sector and is competitive with the cost in China and Vietnam, the quality of the chairs is lower and unsuitable for export.

Several factors prevent Zambia's wood products industry from achieving international competitiveness, including low labor productivity and low capacity utilization, the high cost of wood, poor managerial and worker skills, old technology, weak supply chains, and market segmentation.

Low Labor Productivity and Low Capacity Utilization

Even in larger wood product firms in Zambia, labor productivity is low. The number of chairs produced per worker per day averages 3–6 in China and 2 in Vietnam, but only 0.2–0.6 in Zambia (0.2–0.4 in Ethiopia and 0.3–0.7 in Tanzania; see table 7.1). While wages are lower in Zambia than in China, the difference is not sufficient to compensate for Zambia's lower productivity: the total labor cost per chair in Zambia is more than four times that in China. Similarly, capacity utilization is low: a maximum of 68 percent in Zambia compared with 85–100 percent in China (table 7.1).

The High Cost of Wood

Wood from legal sources is expensive in Zambia, and the cost is passed through the value chain. For example, pine lumber costs $394 per cubic meter in Zambia compared with $344 in China, $275 in Tanzania, and $146–246 in Vietnam (but $667 in Ethiopia). This is largely the result of the monopoly of the Zambia Forestry and Forest Industries Corporation (ZAFFICO) over managed forests and its control over the roundwood price. The other option is to buy wood from the open areas, where sales must be negotiated with the local tribal chiefs. In both cases, the additional commitment fees, associated stipulations and purchase requirements (for ZAFFICO), and royalty fees (for open areas) drive up the price.

Moreover, poor primary processing technology leads to low recovery rates and, thus, higher costs, and poor road infrastructure raises transportation costs.

Table 7.1 Wooden Chair Production: Benchmarking Selected Variables, Five Countries

Indicator	Zambia	China	Vietnam	Ethiopia	Tanzania
Wages, average per month, US$					
Skilled	200–265	383–442	181–259	81–119	150–200
Unskilled	100–160	206–251	85–135	37–52	75–125
Labor productivity, chairs per person per day	0.2–0.6	3.0–6.0	1.2–2.6	0.2–0.4	0.3–0.7
Labor cost per chair, US$	9	2	3	10	19
Cost of lumber (pine), US$ per cubic meter	394	344	146–246	667	275
Cost of consumables (glue, varnish, and so on), US$ per chair	4.30	0.51	1.48	4.22	5.10
Capacity utilization, %	40–68	85–100	60–85	30–80	50–60
Production cost per chair, US$	14.91–30.97	11.46–14.49	13.29–22.52	32.06–49.48	30.00–33.42

Source: GDS 2011.

Light Manufacturing in Zambia • http://dx.doi.org/10.1596/978-0-8213-9935-4

Transportation costs for lumber in Zambia can be as high as $4.25 per kilometer-ton compared with $0.28 in China and even less in the other countries (World Bank 2011). Availability is another concern. Wood processors fear that unregulated or illegal hardwood logging (for exports or as a source of domestic fuel), left unchecked, could exhaust hardwood supplies in Zambia within a few years (Chaponda 2010). Importing wood from abroad is also expensive because of international transportation costs and a 25 percent import duty on roundwood and sawn wood.

Production costs per chair are also high (see figures 7.2 and 7.3). Excluding the cost of lumber, they are 10 times higher in Zambia than in China. Contributing factors are poor managerial and worker skills, outdated technology, and weak supply chains (see below).

Figure 7.2 Cost and Composition of Major Inefficiencies in Wooden Chair Production, China and Zambia

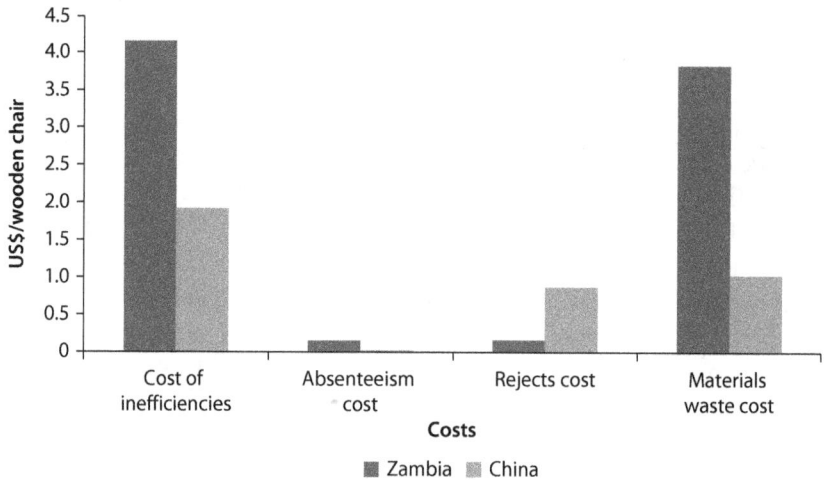

Source: GDS 2011.

Figure 7.3 The Value Chain of Wooden Chairs, Zambia

Local market wooden chair, Un-upholstered   Lusaka, Zambia

Unit production cost $30.97   Lumber price ($/m³) $394 Skilled: unskilled worker ratio 1.5:1

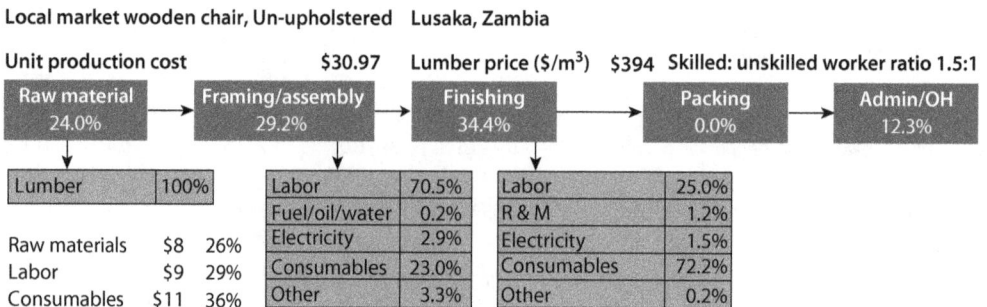

| Raw material 24.0% | Framing/assembly 29.2% | Finishing 34.4% | Packing 0.0% | Admin/OH 12.3% |

Lumber	100%

Raw materials	$8	26%
Labor	$9	29%
Consumables	$11	36%

Labor	70.5%
Fuel/oil/water	0.2%
Electricity	2.9%
Consumables	23.0%
Other	3.3%

Labor	25.0%
R & M	1.2%
Electricity	1.5%
Consumables	72.2%
Other	0.2%

Source: GDS 2011.
Note: OH = overhead; R & M = repair and maintenance costs.

Light Manufacturing in Zambia • http://dx.doi.org/10.1596/978-0-8213-9935-4

Figure 7.4 The Value Chain of Wooden Chairs, China

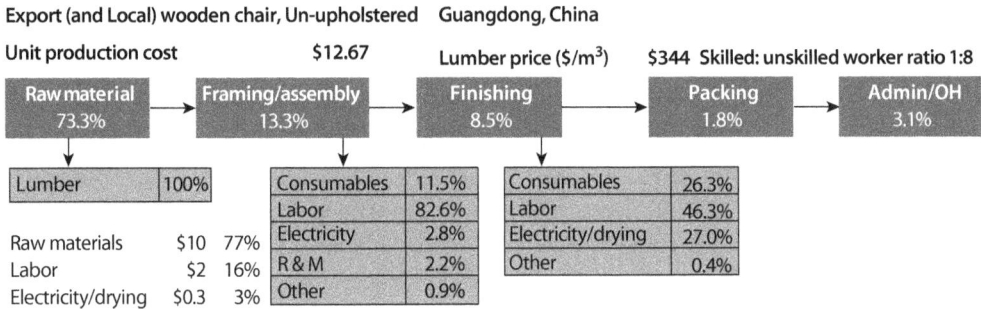

Export (and Local) wooden chair, Un-upholstered   Guangdong, China

Unit production cost $12.67   Lumber price ($/m³) $344 Skilled: unskilled worker ratio 1:8

| Raw material 73.3% | → | Framing/assembly 13.3% | → | Finishing 8.5% | → | Packing 1.8% | → | Admin/OH 3.1% |

Lumber	100%

Consumables	11.5%
Labor	82.6%
Electricity	2.8%
R & M	2.2%
Other	0.9%

Consumables	26.3%
Labor	46.3%
Electricity/drying	27.0%
Other	0.4%

Raw materials	$10	77%
Labor	$2	16%
Electricity/drying	$0.3	3%

Source: GDS 2011.
Note: OH = overhead; R & M = repair and maintenance costs.

Poor Managerial and Worker Skills

The poor management of the production process and inadequately trained workers are reflected in low-quality products, low labor productivity, and the wasteful use of expensive consumables. For example, the production of a chair involves nearly nine times more varnish and finishing oils in Zambia than in China (see table 7.1). Similarly, while Chinese firms waste about 10 percent of the lumber in manufacturing a chair, Zambian firms waste 1.5–3.0 times more. Small and medium firms, which make up more than 95 percent of the registered wood processing companies, struggle to produce high-quality products suitable for export: they produce less than 10 percent of Zambia's wood product exports. The lack of technical expertise in product design and development compounds the problem.

Zambian workers lack basic education, as well as more specific technical and managerial expertise. The Zambia business survey found that a lack of education among micro, small, and medium enterprise workers is associated with lower productivity (Clarke and others 2010), and another survey found that 37 percent of Zambian workers had no education compared with 5 percent or fewer in China, Ethiopia, Tanzania, and Vietnam (World Bank 2011). The latter survey also highlighted problems with management. Among the five countries in our study, Zambia has the smallest share of production workers and the largest share of managers (a 27 percent manager to worker ratio, compared with 16 percent in China and as little as 4 percent in Vietnam). This suggests that labor management may be more difficult in Zambia, requiring more managers for a given number of production workers.

Outdated Technology

Equipment is considerably older, on average, in Zambia than in China and Vietnam, at 28 years compared with 3–7 years in China and 7–13 in Vietnam (GDS 2011). High interest rates and high collateral requirements make it difficult for smaller firms to invest in the technological upgrades needed to increase productivity and product quality. As a result, production costs are high and productivity and quality low.

The survey of small and medium firms found average interest rates of 21 percent in Zambia compared with 10–14 percent in Ethiopia, Tanzania, and Vietnam and less than 5 percent in China. Smaller firms are also disadvantaged by considerably higher collateral requirements in Zambia relative to firms in China (Fafchamps and Quinn 2012). Half the firms surveyed had purchased new equipment, machinery, or vehicles in the previous three years, but most recent purchases (86 percent) had been funded through retained earnings and only 4 percent through loans from financial institutions. While more than half the firms said they could borrow from financial institutions to purchase equipment, it is not clear whether the firms could actually borrow, but chose not to or whether their expectation of being able to borrow was wrong (Fafchamps and Quinn 2012). In-depth interviews of wood product manufacturers identified lack of capital as a constraint on the purchase of modern equipment.

Weak Supply Chains
The shortage of reliable local suppliers of inputs forces furniture producers to backward-integrate into wood preparation and drying. This is a subscale and expensive solution that also creates entry barriers for skilled artisans.

Market Segmentation
The large informal sector is able to produce at lower cost, as little as one-third the cost of production in the formal sector. This is because informal enterprises benefit from lower overhead, the possibility of evading taxes and fees, the use of manual tools (hence, lower capital and electricity costs) and in many cases, access to illegally obtained wood. The outcome is a lower-quality product but one that nonetheless appeals to a large segment of the domestic market (where price is the key consideration). However, this separation of markets and the lack of a sophisticated local market that demands high-quality products reduce the competitive pressure for local manufacturers to improve the quality of their products and is another factor preventing Zambia's wood products sector from becoming internationally competitive.

Recommendations

There are few, if any, short- to medium-term strategies available to make Zambia's wood products sector internationally competitive. Improved competitiveness requires long-term upgrades to formal sector production, greater mechanization, and training in complementary skills. Otherwise, small informal wood manufacturers will remain in a low-level equilibrium of low productivity, low prices, and low income. In the medium term, the wood products sector is expected to focus primarily on the domestic market, and small firms are expected to account for most employment in the sector.

Our main recommendations, to be pursued in parallel, are as follows:

* *Improve competition and efficiency in the supply of wood:* Improving competitiveness will require curtailing illegal trade, providing alternatives to

ZAFFICO's monopoly, and removing distortions in the market to be able to exploit Zambia's high-quality wood sustainably at lower cost. This last could involve encouragement for investment in private wood plantations (which China, Tanzania, and Vietnam have all done successfully) close to the main production and demand centers of the country to minimize transport costs. In the past, there have been concerns about a shortage of plantation roundwood and about inadequate private sector investment in forestry plantations (Mwitwa 2009).

- *Encourage foreign investment in furniture manufacturing:* Foreign investment could bring new technology and management skills to help improve productivity and quality.

- *Develop plug-and-play industrial parks and facilitate clustering:* Establishing industrial parks could improve the access of smaller firms to utilities, land, finance (using land and machines as collateral), and skills (technical assistance programs, particularly targeted at managers). To improve the efficiency of the supply chain, the parks could incorporate a hardwood drying plant supported through a public-private partnership so that individual producers would not need to invest in expensive subscale drying facilities. This would also strengthen the incentive to use legally logged hardwood. Because foreign investors have exhibited limited interest in the sector, the government and domestic investors will need to step up. A major policy challenge for the government is to find ways to enable informal sector firms, which make up most of the sector, to adopt modern technology and access better information (for example, by helping clusters of informal sector firms specialize, invest, and link up with formal sector firms and markets).

Note

1. UN Comtrade (United Nations Commodity Trade Statistics Database), Statistics Division, Department of Economic and Social Affairs, United Nations, New York, http://comtrade.un.org/db.

References

Chaponda, Abigail. 2010. "Pine Timber Crisis Warning." *Post Online*, Post Newspapers, Lusaka. http://www.postzambia.com/post-read_article.php?articleId=15875.

Clarke, George R. G., Manju K. Shah, Marie S. Juliet Munro, and Roland V. Pearson Jr. 2010. *Zambia Business Survey: The Profile and Productivity of Zambian Businesses.* Zambia Business Forum, Private Sector Development Reform Program (Ministry of Commerce, Trade, and Industry), FinMark Trust, and World Bank, Lusaka.

Fafchamps, Marcel, and Simon Quinn. 2012. "Results of Sample Surveys of Firms." In *Performance of Manufacturing Firms in Africa: An Empirical Analysis*, edited by Hinh T. Dinh and George R. G. Clarke, 139–211. Washington, DC: World Bank.

GDS (Global Development Solutions). 2011. *The Value Chain and Feasibility Analysis; Domestic Resource Cost Analysis*. Vol. 2 of *Light Manufacturing in Africa: Targeted Policies to Enhance Private Investment and Create Jobs*. Washington, DC: World Bank. http://go.worldbank.org/6G2A3TFI20.

Mwitwa, J. P. 2009. "Forestry Sector: Situational Analysis." Ministry of Tourism, Environment and Natural Resources, Lusaka.

World Bank. 2011. *Background Papers*. Vol. 3 of *Light Manufacturing in Africa: Targeted Policies to Enhance Private Investment and Create Jobs*. Washington, DC: World Bank. http://go.worldbank.org/LIX5E1FI90.

CHAPTER 8

Metal Products

Introduction

Zambia is a major mineral producer. It is one of the largest copper producers in the world. Yet, Zambia's metal products sector is small. It uses less than 5 percent of the country's copper output in manufacturing, and most finished goods containing copper are imported. The metal products sector overall has accounted for less than 1 percent of gross domestic product and about 1.6 percent of manufacturing output.[1] In 2009, Zambia exported processed metals worth $9.9 million and imported metal products worth $4.1 million.[2]

The local fabrication of copper products is hampered by small domestic and regional markets, while the manufacture of steel products is constrained by the high cost of steel (almost entirely imported). The cost of steel could be lowered by exploiting local iron ore resources. In the meantime, trade logistics should be improved. With the available raw materials as a foundation, additional improvements in access to technology, finance, and skills could support an expansion of the metal products sector.

Despite Zambia's wealth of natural resources, the supply chain is dependent on imports: imports substitute for the lack of many raw materials (although some local copper and scrap metal are used), basic metal products, and more sophisticated fabricated metal products. Figure 8.1 illustrates the market and institutional support structure of the sector.

Zambia has a small copper fabrication industry that has been growing rapidly, but from a small base. It produces a narrow range of products, mainly for the domestic and regional markets (where it benefits from market proximity). However, even in the region, it faces strong competition from the larger, more well developed industry in South Africa.

Several dozen firms are engaged in copper fabrication in Zambia; they employ fewer than 1,000 people (World Bank 2011a). The largest firm is Metal Fabricators of Zambia, a subsidiary of United States–based General Cable Corporation, which uses Zambian copper to produce wire rod, wire, cable, and other products for the domestic, regional, and international markets. Other formal sector firms include the cast product foundry Non-Ferrous Metal Works

Figure 8.1 The Metal Products Market and Institutional Support Structure, Zambia

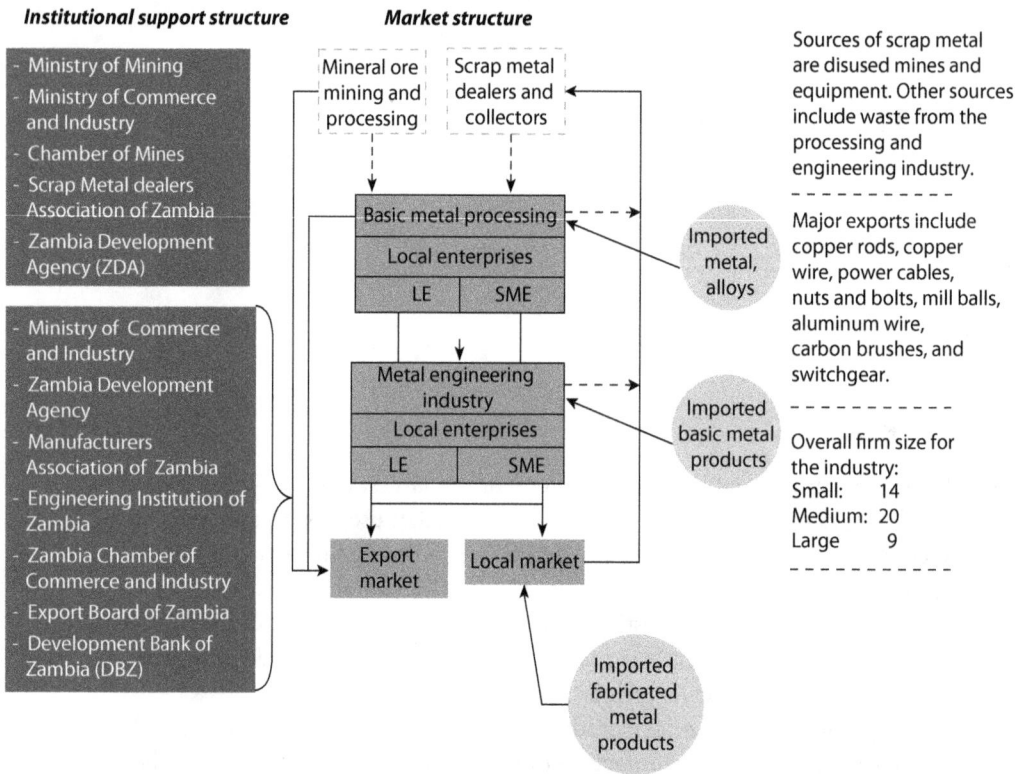

Institutional support structure   *Market structure*

Sources of scrap metal are disused mines and equipment. Other sources include waste from the processing and engineering industry.

- - - - - - - - - -

Major exports include copper rods, copper wire, power cables, nuts and bolts, mill balls, aluminum wire, carbon brushes, and switchgear.

- - - - - - - - - -

Overall firm size for the industry:
Small: 14
Medium: 20
Large   9

- - - - - - - - - -

Institutional support structure (box 1):
- Ministry of Mining
- Ministry of Commerce and Industry
- Chamber of Mines
- Scrap Metal dealers Association of Zambia
- Zambia Development Agency (ZDA)

Institutional support structure (box 2):
- Ministry of Commerce and Industry
- Zambia Development Agency
- Manufacturers Association of Zambia
- Engineering Institution of Zambia
- Zambia Chamber of Commerce and Industry
- Export Board of Zambia
- Development Bank of Zambia (DBZ)

Market structure elements: Mineral ore mining and processing; Scrap metal dealers and collectors; Basic metal processing / Local enterprises (LE, SME); Metal engineering industry / Local enterprises (LE, SME); Export market; Local market; Imported metal, alloys; Imported basic metal products; Imported fabricated metal products.

Source: GDS 2011.

Note: Dashed lines indicate a weak link, lack of organization, and areas where technical support is required to strengthen ties along the supply chain; dotted arrows indicate scrap metal from local companies that is recycled back into the supply chain; LE = large enterprise; SME = small and medium enterprise.

(Zambia) Ltd. and the wire and cable manufacturer Kavino, both largely oriented toward the domestic market. There are also a few informal sector firms that produce relatively simple products for the local market. Many manufacturers of copper-based products in Zambia—both formal and informal—rely on imported raw materials (including copper) or scrap. El Sewedy Transformers, which manufactures electrical transformers for the local market, imports all its copper (reportedly because Zambian suppliers cannot meet its needs). Similarly, most of the decorative copper products sold in Zambia are produced in Zimbabwe from copper sheets imported from Europe (World Bank 2011a).

The steel products sector counts 43 registered small, medium, and large companies and employs some 2,360 people. Among these companies, indigenous Zambian firms produce a few poor-quality metal products (candle holders, chicken feeders, buckets, door frames); formal sector firms produce import-competitive products (such as metal roofing, nails, steel balls, and rails); and a single large firm that runs a positive trade balance produces a few export-competitive products, including crown corks.

The production of roofing sheets illustrates the promise of the sector. In recent years, Zambia has experienced a shift from trading in imported sheets toward manufacturing and even exporting the sheets to neighboring countries. Encouraged by a growing construction industry and a favorable business environment, both foreign and Zambian firms have established facilities to manufacture iron roofing sheets in Zambia, with plans to expand.

Several firms have benefited from government support and investment incentives. Metal fabrication has been designated a priority industry for investment incentives. The government recently introduced several measures to support the local iron and steel manufacturing industry. The 2011 national budget increased the customs duty on deformed bars, cold-rolled coils, and galvanized coils to "take cognizance of existing local capacity to produce various steel products" (ZRA 2010, 10). Other measures include a ban on exports of scrap metal and a 25 percent duty on imports of metal products such as grinding mill balls, railway turnouts, and nuts and bolts.[3]

Sectoral Potential

Several factors favor the sector:

- *Zambia's iron ore deposits, together with competitive sources of hydroenergy and an established (copper) mining and smelter tradition:* These factors could enable a competitive steel industry to emerge, especially because of steel's low value-to-weight ratio, which makes imports relatively expensive, even if trade logistics are improved.
- *An established copper mining industry:* The mining industry could serve as a domestic source of the key input for copper fabrication, although the availability of copper locally may not provide as much of an advantage to copper fabricators as might be expected (see below).
- *Potentially high productivity:* Productivity is considerably greater in Zambia than in China in crown cork production, which takes place at a single, well-managed, highly automated firm (table 8.1).
- *A potential local market in the mining and construction industries for many metal products that are currently imported at high cost:* Realizing this potential requires that local products compete on price and quality and that the mines can be persuaded to buy local. Furthermore, Zambia's exports of steel products to neighboring countries suggests that Zambia could also take advantage of regional market opportunities.

Over the long term, growth in the domestic and regional manufacturing sectors could boost the demand for fabricated copper products and support some expansion of Zambia's copper products sector. But even if these opportunities are realized, copper fabrication may not offer the desired socioeconomic benefits, for several reasons. Copper fabrication is a capital-intensive industry; even modest growth would not create a large number of jobs. Copper fabrication is subject

Table 8.1 Crown Cork Production: Benchmarking Selected Variables, Four Countries

Indicator	Zambia[a]	China	Vietnam	Ethiopia
Wages, average per month, US$				
Skilled	510	265–369	168–233	181
Unskilled	342	192–265	117–142	89
Labor productivity, factory level, 1,000 pieces per person per day	201.9	12.9–25.1	24.7–26.7	10.4
Capacity utilization, %	52	95–100	70–100	99
Processing cost, excluding raw materials, US$ per 1,000 pieces	0.60	0.60	0.47	0.78
Production cost, US$ per 1,000 pieces	5.67	4.81–5.32	4.43–5.01	6.91
Average selling price, US$ per 1,000 pieces				
Factory gate	6.79	5.75–6.64	5.13–5.80	8.64
Free on board	—	6.19–7.08	—	—

Source: GDS 2011.

Note: — = not available.

a. Data for Zambia are from a single, well-managed, highly automated firm.

to the same demand and price cycle as refined copper and may not be a good source of economic diversification. And copper fabrication is not a high-margin industry: the margins are lower in copper fabrication than in copper mining and refining.[4]

A detailed value chain analysis of crown corks suggests that Zambia may have potential in the manufacture of steel products, especially for domestic and regional markets. The domestic resource cost ratio for crown corks is 0.68 (a ratio below 1 indicates a potential comparative advantage; see chapter 1), and Zambia is already exporting this product to other countries in the region (World Bank 2011b).

The crown corks produced in Zambia are more expensive than those produced in China and Vietnam, but cost less than those produced in Ethiopia and are competitive in the region (see table 8.1). This is so despite the higher cost of labor in Zambia, at almost three times the cost of skilled workers in Ethiopia and almost four times the cost of unskilled workers; wages are also higher than in China and Vietnam. Zambia's regional competitiveness in crown corks, despite the higher wages, derives from the high level of automation, which boosts labor productivity.

The Main Constraints on Competitiveness

There are four key drivers of success in metal fabrication in Zambia, and each is constrained in some way: access to raw materials (copper, alloying materials, and scrap metal), capital, skilled labor, and markets. Table 8.2 shows how Zambia performs on each driver of success in copper and steel products.

Many of the constraints affecting the metal products industry are similar to those affecting light industry in general: poor managerial and technical skills and a lack of high-quality equipment. These constraints especially affect small and

Table 8.2 Advantages and Disadvantages in the Fabrication of Copper and Steel Products, Zambia, 2010

Driver	Copper products	Steel products
Access to raw materials	? Copper is available locally, but this is not a major advantage because copper cathode is available at the same price all over the world; the maximum saving from procuring copper locally is the transport cost, and that is likely to be offset by the cost of shipping the final product abroad. ✗ Most alloying metals are not available locally and would have to be imported. ✗ Scrap is in small supply locally.	✗ Steel must be imported, at high cost. ✓ Iron ore deposits, hydroenergy availability, and an established (copper) mining and smelter tradition could enable the development of a competitive steel industry.
Access to capital	? Not a major problem for large international firms, but difficult for small and medium enterprises.	? Not a major problem for large international firms, but difficult for small and medium enterprises.
Access to skilled labor	✗ Difficult, especially for small and medium enterprises.	✗ Difficult, especially for small and medium enterprises.
Access to markets	✗ Small domestic and regional markets for fabricated copper products (excluding South Africa, which is largely self-sufficient). ✗ Access to international markets is hindered by poor transport, poor trade logistics, and competition from other fabricators located closer to markets.	✓ Good domestic and regional markets (for example, the mining industry).

Sources: Copper products: World Bank 2011a; steel products: GDS 2011.
Note: ✓ = advantage; ✗ = disadvantage; ? = conditional.

medium enterprises. In addition, inadequate demand and high costs constrain the industry.

The Inadequate Demand for Copper Products

The domestic and regional demand for fabricated copper products is insufficient to support any large expansion of Zambia's copper fabrication industry (World Bank 2011a). This disadvantage outweighs the limited advantage of the local availability of copper ore. While there is a large international market for fabricated copper products, Zambia would have difficulty competing because of high transport costs and poor trade logistics, as well as strong competition from Asian fabricators located closer to international markets and from South African firms with lower transport costs to non-African markets. If Zambia can address the transport and logistics costs, it can gain market share in world markets because of its otherwise favorable cost structure.

The High Cost of Steel

The mining and construction industries are a potential local market for many metal products that are currently imported at high cost, provided that local producers can compete on price and quality and that the mines can be persuaded to buy local (Kaiser Associates 2011). The minister of commerce, trade, and industry recently stated that growth in the mining sector—the country's biggest user of steel and iron products—has not translated into similar growth in the local steel and iron industry because mining companies prefer imported products (Chulu and Wangwe 2011).

The high price of steel in Zambia—almost 50 percent higher than in China (tin-free steel costs $1,610 per ton in Zambia compared with $1,106 in China)—serves as a major disadvantage to Zambian metal products manufacturers (figures 8.2 and 8.3). Imported steel accounts for nearly 60 percent of the total production cost of crown corks, for example. This disadvantage outweighs the advantage arising from higher labor productivity in Zambia and more than explains the 7 percent higher production cost of crown corks in Zambia relative to China. The high cost of steel in Zambia results from the need to transport this bulky item over long distances (high transport costs and poor trade logistics) and from the 20 percent import tariff. The government

Figure 8.2 The Crown Cork Value Chain, Zambia

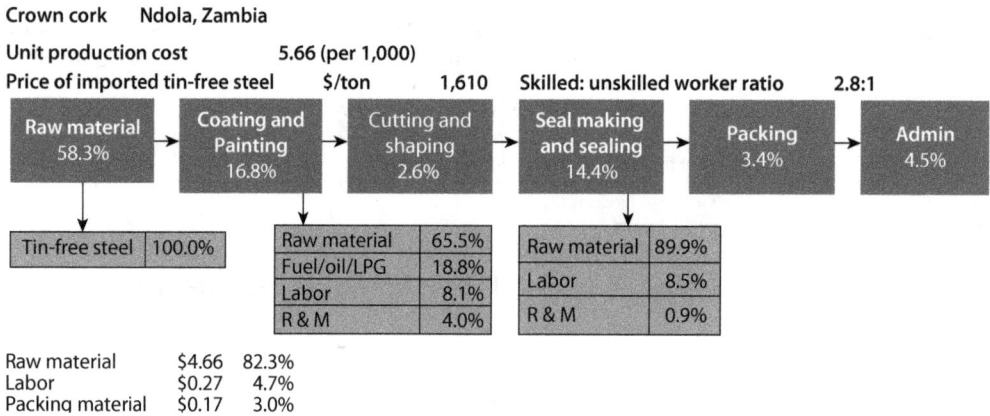

Crown cork   Ndola, Zambia

Unit production cost   5.66 (per 1,000)
Price of imported tin-free steel $/ton   1,610   Skilled: unskilled worker ratio   2.8:1

| Raw material 58.3% | Coating and Painting 16.8% | Cutting and shaping 2.6% | Seal making and sealing 14.4% | Packing 3.4% | Admin 4.5% |

Tin-free steel	100.0%

Raw material	65.5%
Fuel/oil/LPG	18.8%
Labor	8.1%
R & M	4.0%

Raw material	89.9%
Labor	8.5%
R & M	0.9%

Raw material	$4.66	82.3%
Labor	$0.27	4.7%
Packing material	$0.17	3.0%

Source: GDS 2011.
Note: LPG = liquefied petroleum gas; R & M = repair and maintenance costs.

Figure 8.3 The Crown Cork Value Chain, China

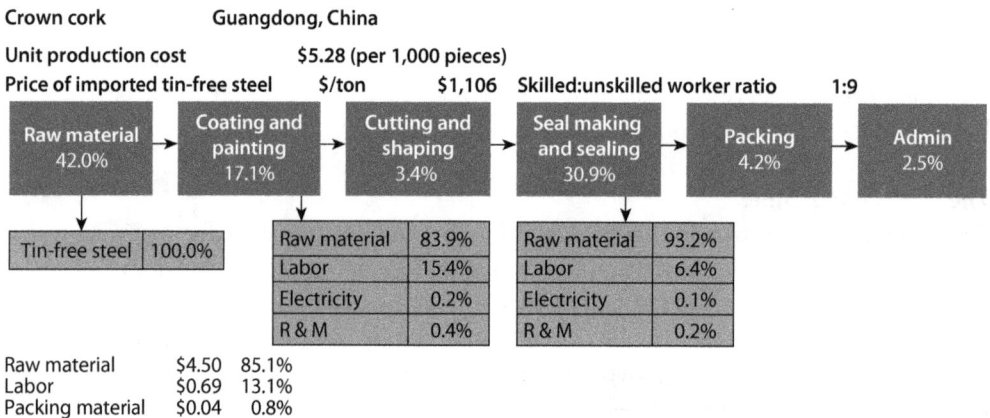

Crown cork   Guangdong, China

Unit production cost $5.28 (per 1,000 pieces)
Price of imported tin-free steel $/ton $1,106   Skilled:unskilled worker ratio   1:9

| Raw material 42.0% | Coating and painting 17.1% | Cutting and shaping 3.4% | Seal making and sealing 30.9% | Packing 4.2% | Admin 2.5% |

Tin-free steel	100.0%

Raw material	83.9%
Labor	15.4%
Electricity	0.2%
R & M	0.4%

Raw material	93.2%
Labor	6.4%
Electricity	0.1%
R & M	0.2%

Raw material	$4.50	85.1%
Labor	$0.69	13.1%
Packing material	$0.04	0.8%

Source: GDS 2011.
Note: R & M = repair and maintenance costs.

recently banned exports of scrap metal to create reserves of raw material for local iron and steel manufacturers.[5]

Despite this cost disadvantage, Zambia still manages to be regionally competitive in the production of crown corks. For example, while the cost of tin-free steel is 14 percent higher in Zambia than in Ethiopia and labor costs are also considerably higher, the unit cost of crown cork production is 18 percent lower in Zambia. The difference is attributable largely to the high degree of automation and, hence, to high labor productivity and low materials waste. Capacity utilization for the lone crown cork plant in Zambia is only 52 percent; yet, the plant meets more than 75 percent of the local market demand. The firm would benefit greatly from access to export markets.

Recommendations

The following recommendations for resolving the key constraints in the metal products sector relate mainly to steel products. Because of the market constraints faced by the copper fabrication industry, it is difficult to pinpoint specific policies that would have a major impact on the industry's competitiveness in the short term. Nonetheless, the longer-term development of the industry could be promoted through policies to encourage the manufacturing sector more broadly and thereby gradually build local demand for fabricated copper products.

- *Improve access to reasonably priced steel by*
  - *Eliminating the 20 percent import tariff on steel* (with little fiscal impact; see below): This would save an estimated $0.40 in the production cost of 1,000 crown corks.
  - *Improving transport and trade logistics:* This could halve the transportation cost of steel, saving $100 per ton, for a savings of $0.20 on 1,000 crown corks. It could also lower the cost of some noncopper inputs in the copper fabrication industry and lessen Zambia's disadvantage in accessing international markets for fabricated products. Two priority actions are required: streamlining the procedure for obtaining letters of credit and reducing border waiting times (for example, by establishing one-stop border posts). Rail is often cheaper than trucks for transporting heavy, bulky goods such as minerals and steel, and many believe that revitalizing Zambia's rail system (as well as the rail link between Zambia and Dar es Salaam) could assist these industries.[6] Because an upgraded rail system would face strong competition from Zambia's competitive trucking industry, efforts to invest in rail should be viewed in the context of a broader, multimodal transport network (Raballand and Whitworth 2011). Investments in rail are likely to be more effective if they come from the private sector (such as the plans of Universal Mining and Chemical Industries to construct a railway line to transport iron ore and steel from its mines and processing facilities).[7] The government would play a facilitating role. The government also has an

important role in establishing a conducive policy environment, upgrading and maintaining key truck roads, and ensuring that the costs of road maintenance are fully recovered through appropriate road user charges and fuel taxes (Raballand and Whitworth 2011).

- *Enabling the exploitation of local iron ore deposits:* Zambia has known iron ore deposits of more than 600 million tons, and there is much interest in exploiting them. Universal Mining and Chemical Industries is said to be planning to invest more than $130 million in developing two iron ore mines to supply its steel plant and avoid an anticipated shortage of scrap metal.[8] Over the longer term, the combination of untapped competitive iron ore deposits and low-cost hydroelectricity could eliminate the cost disadvantage associated with imported steel. An in-depth feasibility study should be undertaken to assess the potential competitiveness of a domestic steel industry.
- *Consider providing small and medium firms with government-facilitated (but not subsidized) direct procurement of duty-free steel imports:* This could be accomplished as part of an incubator program (see below).

- *Facilitate access to advanced technologies:* Zambia has emerged as a regional competitor in crown corks thanks to the high level of automation and the use of high-technology machinery. Copper fabrication firms (especially smaller ones) are disadvantaged by their lack of access to financing for suitable equipment (World Bank 2011a). Expanding access to technology could help Zambia become more competitive in metal products. For example, Scaw Ltd., one of the main manufacturers of steel products in Zambia, plans a $15 million recapitalization program to develop capacity to manufacture forged steel balls rather than cast balls. Scaw intends to expand its market share by providing the higher-quality steel balls that are currently being imported (Kaiser Associates 2011). Involving foreign investors could help in transferring technology, and the government is seeking investors for a foundry to produce world-class mill balls and mill liners (ZDA and CBC 2011). However, highly automated capital-intensive processes such as crown cork production provide only a limited opportunity for employment growth.

- *Develop plug-and-play industrial parks:* Industrial parks would facilitate the access of small and medium metal product fabricators to utilities, land, finance (using land and machines as collateral), and skills. A 2009 nationally representative survey of Zambian small and medium enterprises found that lack of access to utilities, finance, and education is associated with low productivity (Clarke and others 2010). These constraints have also been identified as both direct and indirect checks on the development of copper fabrication in Zambia (see World Bank 2011a).

- *Establish a business incubator for informal, indigenous firms:* International experience has demonstrated the utility of incubator programs, while a survey of Zambian micro, small, and medium firms has found that training and the development of business networks could increase their efficiency and competitiveness (Conway and Shah 2010). In conjunction with an industrial park, a business incubator could meet several of the following needs:

- *Information:* A relatively low-cost information package might include details on product specifications and prices, as well as sources of the steel and machinery required and the distribution outlets that sell the products.
- *Training:* If a critical mass of technical capabilities can be developed in the metals industry, spillovers in the form of a more well-trained cadre of workers and firm owners could motivate formal sector metal firms to outsource and diversify into more products, possibly for export. Options include technical assistance programs, particularly for firm managers, and perhaps including kaizen training; firm-financed, machine-specific training provided by equipment suppliers; the use of extension workers to conduct regular on-site visits to assess the evolving needs of smaller firms and provide hands-on assistance; and trade schools to provide subsidized technical training (perhaps established and operated through collaboration among developing countries, but requiring public investment).[9]
- *Access to raw materials and equipment:* Access to inputs and equipment could be improved through government-facilitated imports of steel and of machinery.
- *Marketing support:* The government could subsidize advertising for the new products produced in the incubators. Certification that Zambian metal products meet international quality standards could also improve marketing, and the government may be able to assist firms with certification. An absence of such certification may be constraining sales of Zambian-made steel products to the mines (Macsteel Exports 2010).
- *Networking opportunities:* Business and social networks and backward and forward links could be established.

Notes

1. Data of the Zambia Central Statistical Office and the Ministry of Commerce, Trade, and Industry.
2. UN Comtrade (United Nations Commodity Trade Statistics Database), Statistics Division, Department of Economic and Social Affairs, United Nations, New York, http://comtrade.un.org/db.
3. "Zambia Government Gives Incentives to Steel Industry," *Post*, Lusaka, Zambia, July 6, 2011.
4. The world's largest copper producer, Chile, has also not developed into a major fabricator on a global scale. Rather than investing heavily in fabrication, Chile has capitalized on its resource base by establishing a competitive mining industry, ensuring that the benefits of copper are channeled to the population, and encouraging diversification in industries with growth potential (such as horticulture, fisheries, and tourism). Chile's fabrication meets the needs of local industry and infrastructure, but little else (World Bank 2011a).
5. "RB Bans Export of Scrap Metal," *Lusaka Times*, Lusaka, Zambia, September 20, 2011.

6. For example, see the comments by the Chamber of Mines of Zambia and the Zambia Chambers of Commerce and Industry in "Revisit RSZ Concession: ZACCI," *Times of Zambia*, Ndola, Zambia, February 4, 2010; see also MOF (2011).

7. See "Universal Mining Invest USD 130 Million in Zambia," *SteelGuru*, New Delhi, http://www.steelguru.com/raw_material_news/Universal_Mining_invest_USD_130_million_in_Zambia/190119.html.

8. See State House (2011); "Universal Mining Stakes K250 Billion," *Times of Zambia*, Ndola, Zambia, July 22, 2011.

9. Kaizen training conducted as part of this study was found to have a highly significant impact on marketing and other business practices in Ethiopia's metalworking industry (see World Bank 2011c).

References

Chulu, Kabanda, and Misheck Wangwe. 2011. "Govt Gives Incentives to Steel, Pharmaceutical Industries." *Post Online*, Post Newspapers, Lusaka. http://www.postzambia.com/post-read_article.php?articleId=21715.

Clarke, George R. G., Manju K. Shah, Marie Sheppard, Juliet Munro, and Roland V. Pearson, Jr. 2010. "Zambia Business Survey: The Profile and Productivity of Zambian Businesses." Zambia Business Forum, Private Sector Development Reform Program (Ministry of Commerce, Trade, and Industry), FinMark Trust, and World Bank, Lusaka.

Conway, Patrick, and Manju K. Shah. 2010. *Zambia Business Survey: Who's Productive in Zambia's Private Sector? Evidence from the Zambia Business Survey*. Zambia Business Forum, Private Sector Development Reform Program (Ministry of Commerce, Trade, and Industry), FinMark Trust, and World Bank, Lusaka.

GDS (Global Development Solutions). 2011. *The Value Chain and Feasibility Analysis; Domestic Resource Cost Analysis*. Vol. 2 of *Light Manufacturing in Africa: Targeted Policies to Enhance Private Investment and Create Jobs*. Washington, DC: World Bank. http://go.worldbank.org/6G2A3TFI20.

Kaiser Associates. 2011. *Supply Linkages between Mines and Local Suppliers in Zambia*. Draft report, World Bank, Washington, DC.

Macsteel Exports. 2010. "Get International Certification." News release, Macsteel Exports, Johannesburg, September 28. http://www.macsteelexports.com/news/get-international-certification.

MOF (Zambia, Ministry of Finance and National Planning). 2011. *Sixth National Development Plan 2011–2015: "Sustained Economic Growth and Poverty Reduction."* Lusaka: MOF.

Raballand, Gaël, and Alan Whitworth. 2011. "Should the Zambian Government Invest in Railways?" ZIPAR Working Paper 3, Zambia Institute for Policy Analysis and Research, Lusaka.

State House, Office of the President of Zambia. 2011. "Iron Mine, Mumbwa-Lusaka Rail to Gobble $130 Million." State House, Lusaka, March 14.

World Bank. 2011a. "What Is the Potential for More Copper Fabrication in Zambia?" Report 62379-ZM, Finance and Private Sector Development Unit, Africa Region, World Bank, Washington, DC.

————. 2011b. *Background Papers.* Vol. 3 of *Light Manufacturing in Africa: Targeted Policies to Enhance Private Investment and Create Jobs.* Washington, DC: World Bank. http://go.worldbank.org/LIX5E1FI90.

————. 2011c. *Kaizen for Managerial Skills Improvement in Small and Medium Enterprises: An Impact Evaluation Study.* Vol. 4 of *Light Manufacturing in Africa: Targeted Policies to Enhance Private Investment and Create Jobs.* Washington, DC: World Bank. http://go.worldbank.org/4Y1QF5FIB0.

ZDA (Zambia Development Agency) and CBC (Commonwealth Business Council). 2011. "Investment Project Profiles." Zambia Investment Forum, Lusaka.

ZRA (Zambia Revenue Authority). 2010. "2011 Budget Overview of Tax Changes." Sections 3.2.2 and 3.2.3, ZRA, Lusaka. http://www.zra.org.zm/2011BudgetHighlights.pdf.

CHAPTER 9

Agribusiness

Introduction

The Sixth National Development Plan (SNDP) considers agriculture "the priority sector in achieving sustainable economic growth and reducing poverty in Zambia" (MOF 2011, 108). Indeed, because the climate is favorable and only 15 percent of agricultural land is under cultivation, Zambia's agricultural potential is substantial. Yet, both primary agriculture and agribusiness are underperforming.

Most production costs in agribusiness are associated with raw materials. Consequently, the actions that are most critical to any effort to improve Zambia's competitiveness in agribusiness are at the agricultural production end of the supply chain: reducing the cost of growing crops and rearing livestock and enhancing agricultural productivity.

This chapter relies on a detailed analysis of the value chains for two products—wheat flour and processed milk—to draw implications for the wider agribusiness sector.

In 2008, the agriculture sector accounted for about 20 percent of Zambia's gross domestic product, 9 percent of total exports, and 47 percent of nontraditional exports. The sector is the largest employer in Zambia, absorbing some two-thirds of the labor force, making it the main source of income and employment for the majority of Zambians in rural and periurban areas. Most agricultural enterprises and workers (85 percent) operate in the informal sector (GDS 2011).

Primary agricultural products, mainly tobacco, maize, coffee, and tea, accounted for more than half of Zambian agricultural exports over 2004–08. Zambia imported $182 million in processed foods in 2009.[1] Agroprocessing industries that depend directly on agriculture constitute around 60 percent of Zambia's manufacturing.

Among developing countries, Zambia is one of the largest producers of wheat flour. It exported around $20 million worth in 2009 (almost one-third of the exports of wheat flour by least developed countries).[2] According to the Food and Agriculture Organization of the United Nations, Zambia produced an estimated 84,000 tons of milk in 2008.[3] The country runs a large trade deficit in dairy products: it exported approximately $242,000 worth of dairy products in 2009, but imported 20 times more.[4]

Sectoral Potential

Based on a domestic resource cost estimate, Zambia's competitiveness in wheat milling is highly sensitive to the assumed selling price. While Zambia is currently a net exporter (regionally) of wheat, its export price is well above the cost, insurance, and freight price for wheat from China and the domestic price in Ethiopia and is unlikely to be sustainable (for more, see GDS 2011). Sustained competitiveness in wheat milling will require a reorganization of some markets (for example, fertilizer) and even a major restructuring to bring costs down to the level of costs in other economies in the region.

The wider agribusiness sector has strong potential, provided action is taken to reduce production costs and increase productivity. Growth in the sector could have a major positive impact on the livelihoods of a large number of Zambians in rural areas.[5]

There is a clear opportunity to expand Zambia's agribusiness sector, based on the following factors:

- The potential is strong for the domestic production of primary agricultural products as inputs for the agroprocessing sector:
  - Climate and soil are favorable: 58 percent of the country's land area is classified as medium- to high-potential land for agricultural production. Yet, much of it is uncultivated, and much of the land that is cultivated shows relatively low yields (MOAC and MOLF 2010).
  - Several agricultural products are well established, and there is potential for increasing productivity and production. Some products, such as wheat, cotton, and coffee, are already being exported.
  - A large share of the population is accustomed to an agricultural way of life and to rearing cattle and is available to work in agriculture and animal husbandry. Around two-thirds of the labor force is engaged in low-productivity agriculture, and the vast majority of micro, small, and medium enterprises are agriculture based.
- Rising incomes, urbanization, and changing consumption patterns could drive growth in the domestic demand for processed foods. Many processed food products are imported, and, while the per capita consumption of many processed foods such as milk is low, there is a strong growth potential.

The Main Constraints on Competitiveness

The main constraint faced by agribusiness in Zambia is the high cost of inputs, that is, the outputs of the agricultural industry.[6] For both wheat flour and processed milk, raw materials account for a high proportion of the production costs (see figures 9.1–9.4, including the value chain analysis for China for comparison).

For example, for wheat flour, raw materials (almost all wheat) account for more than 85 percent of the production costs. The situation is similar for several other processed agricultural products.

Despite favorable soil and climate and wheat yields in line with those in China and six times those in Ethiopia, wheat and raw milk are expensive in Zambia. A ton of domestically produced wheat costs $400–500, compared with around $200 in China and Vietnam and around $350 in Ethiopia and Tanzania (table 9.1). Because imported wheat costs even more, Zambian mills tend to use domestic wheat. The cost of raw milk is 50 percent higher (perhaps more) in Zambia than in China and Vietnam (table 9.2). A large proportion of the cost of the raw milk is for feed, which is expensive (15 percent more expensive in

Figure 9.1 Wheat Milling Value Chain, Zambia

Wheat milling   Chisamba, Zambia
Unit production cost ($/ton) $730
Price of wheat $/ton   Domestic $500
Additional income from sales of bran ($/ton) $89   Skilled: unskilled worker ratio   1:5

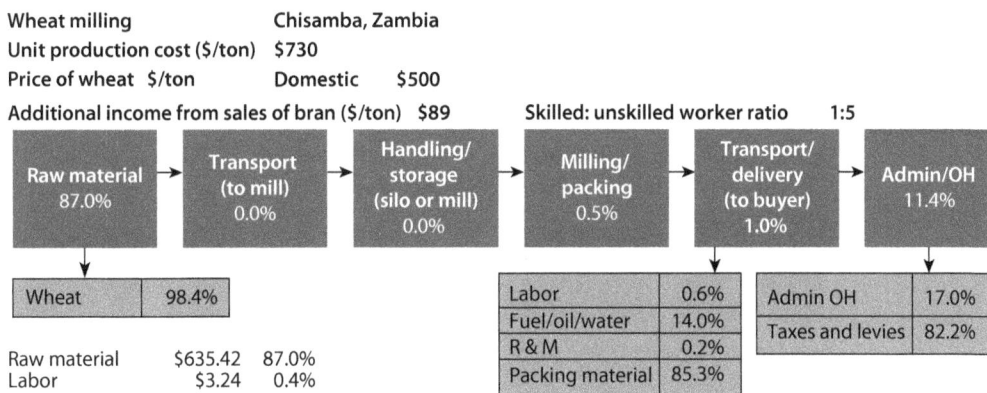

| Raw material 87.0% | → | Transport (to mill) 0.0% | → | Handling/ storage (silo or mill) 0.0% | → | Milling/ packing 0.5% | → | Transport/ delivery (to buyer) 1.0% | → | Admin/OH 11.4% |

| Wheat | 98.4% |

Labor	0.6%
Fuel/oil/water	14.0%
R & M	0.2%
Packing material	85.3%

| Admin OH | 17.0% |
| Taxes and levies | 82.2% |

| Raw material | $635.42 | 87.0% |
| Labor | $3.24 | 0.4% |

Source: GDS 2011.
Note: OH = overhead; R & M = repair and maintenance costs.

Figure 9.2 Wheat Milling Value Chain, China

Wheat milling   Jiangsu, China
Unit production cost ($/ton) $322
Price of wheat $/ton $192
Additional income from sales of bran ($/ton) $230   Skilled: unskilled worker ratio   1:9

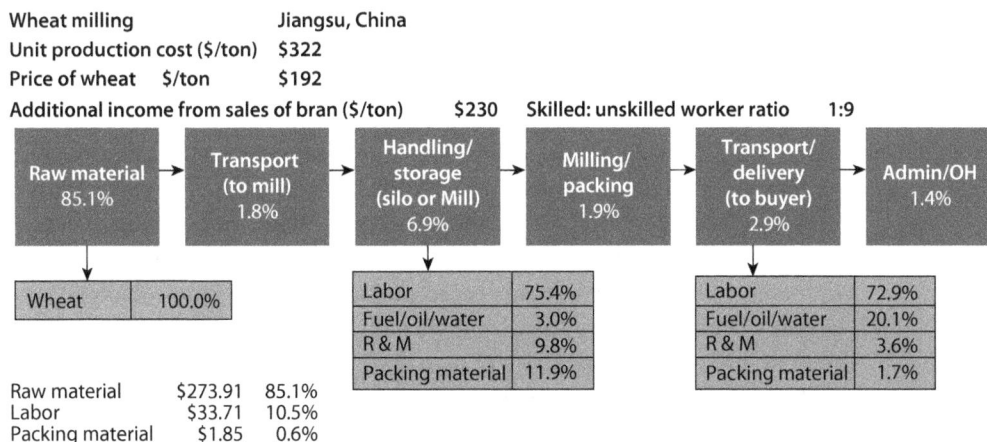

| Raw material 85.1% | → | Transport (to mill) 1.8% | → | Handling/ storage (silo or Mill) 6.9% | → | Milling/ packing 1.9% | → | Transport/ delivery (to buyer) 2.9% | → | Admin/OH 1.4% |

| Wheat | 100.0% |

Labor	75.4%
Fuel/oil/water	3.0%
R & M	9.8%
Packing material	11.9%

Labor	72.9%
Fuel/oil/water	20.1%
R & M	3.6%
Packing material	1.7%

Raw material	$273.91	85.1%
Labor	$33.71	10.5%
Packing material	$1.85	0.6%

Source: GDS 2011.
Note: OH = overhead; R & M = repair and maintenance costs.

Light Manufacturing in Zambia • http://dx.doi.org/10.1596/978-0-8213-9935-4

Figure 9.3 Raw Milk Value Chain, Zambia

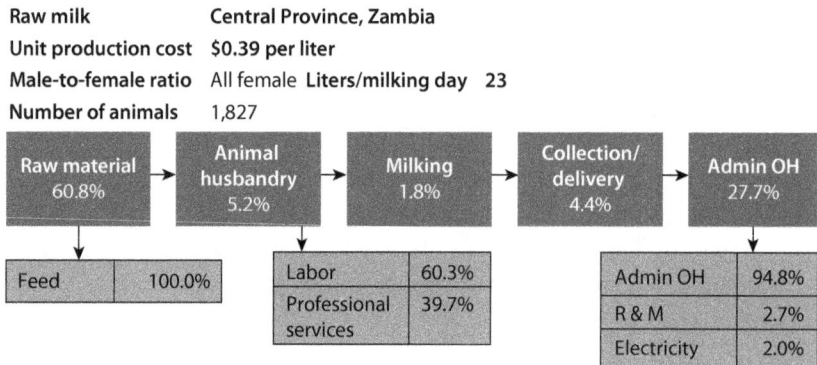

Raw milk   Central Province, Zambia
Unit production cost $0.39 per liter
Male-to-female ratio   All female Liters/milking day   23
Number of animals   1,827

Raw material 60.8%	Animal husbandry 5.2%	Milking 1.8%	Collection/ delivery 4.4%	Admin OH 27.7%

Feed	100.0%

Labor	60.3%
Professional services	39.7%

Admin OH	94.8%
R & M	2.7%
Electricity	2.0%

Source: GDS 2011.
Note: OH = overhead; R & M = repair and maintenance costs.

Figure 9.4 Raw Milk Value Chain, China

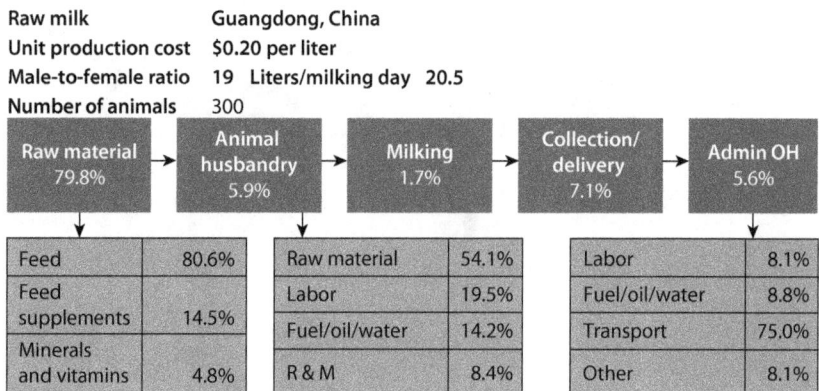

Raw milk   Guangdong, China
Unit production cost $0.20 per liter
Male-to-female ratio   19 Liters/milking day 20.5
Number of animals   300

Raw material 79.8%	Animal husbandry 5.9%	Milking 1.7%	Collection/ delivery 7.1%	Admin OH 5.6%

Feed	80.6%
Feed supplements	14.5%
Minerals and vitamins	4.8%

Raw material	54.1%
Labor	19.5%
Fuel/oil/water	14.2%
R & M	8.4%

Labor	8.1%
Fuel/oil/water	8.8%
Transport	75.0%
Other	8.1%

Source: GDS 2011.
Note: OH = overhead; R & M = repair and maintenance costs.

Zambia than in South Africa, for example) (World Bank 2011a, 2011b). The underlying causes of the high costs of these raw materials are discussed in detail below.

The high cost of the raw materials is compounded by high processing costs. For example, processing 1 ton of wheat into flour (excluding the wheat input and packaging) costs $88 in Zambia, the same as in Vietnam, but 60 percent more than in China and three to four times more than in Ethiopia and Tanzania. Ultimately, wheat flour sells for more than $700 a ton at the factory gate in Zambia, 50 percent more than Ethiopia and Tanzania and almost three times as much as in China (figure 9.5).

The lack of competitiveness has several underlying causes:

• *Imperfections in the markets for key agricultural inputs, agricultural outputs–agroprocessing inputs, and agroprocessing outputs:* An example is the

Table 9.1 Wheat Flour Production: Benchmarking Selected Variables, Five Countries
US$

Indicator	Zambia	China	Vietnam	Ethiopia	Tanzania
Cost of wheat, per ton					
Domestic	400–500	192	269	333	300–365
Imported	—	—	208	304	261–328
Average cost of raw materials, per ton of wheat flour	625	322	323	408	363
Average wage, per month					
Skilled	320–340	398–442	181–363	89–141	200–250
Unskilled	131–149	192–236	78–207	26–52	100–133
Average processing cost, per ton of wheat flour[a]	88	55	89	29	23
Production cost, per ton of wheat flour	662–758	322–377	359–463	415–458	420–512
By-product value, per ton of wheat bran	89	230	259	89	110–150
Average selling price, per ton of wheat flour					
Factory gate	702	228–265	348–404	444–489	435–448
Wholesale	723–943	273–325	390	467–504	448–461
Free on board	—	295–324	—	—	—

Source: GDS 2011.
Note: — = not available.
a. Excluding the wheat input and packaging.

Table 9.2 Dairy Farming: Benchmarking Selected Variables, Five Countries

Indicator	Zambia	China	Vietnam	Ethiopia	Tanzania
Average yield, liters per cow per day	8.0–23.0	20.0–20.5	4.2–15.9	7.0–15.0	2.0–20.0
Average wage, US$ per month					
Skilled	106–340	177–206	—	30–63	150–300
Unskilled	54–181	118–133	31–78	13–41	50–80
Labor productivity, liters per person per day	19.0–179.0	23.5–53.1	2.5–3.9	18.5–71.5	10.0–100.0
Production cost, US$ per liter of milk	0.38–0.45	0.23–0.28	0.09–0.29	0.23–0.47	0.20–0.40
Average selling price, US$ per liter					
Farmgate	0.55–0.64	0.27–0.32	0.38–0.39	0.37–0.44	0.23–0.47
Wholesale	0.64–1.06	0.27–0.32	0.36–0.37	—	0.33–0.60

Source: GDS 2011.
Note: — = not available.

inefficiencies in the land tenure system and in the allocation of land.[7] Other examples include government intervention in the fertilizer market, local government levies on the movement of agricultural produce, and import and export bans on wheat and wheat flour (often imposed without notice, resulting in uncertainty in the market and encouraging smuggling).[8]

- *Other constraints on agricultural production:* The constraints on Zambia's primary agricultural sector are well known and have been described in detail elsewhere (for example, World Bank 2011a). They include the following:
  - *A lack of the domestic production of key inputs, which have to be imported; poor trade logistics; and high transportation and distribution costs:* For example, the cost of inputs critical to the cattle industry—such as feed, breeding supplies,

Figure 9.5 Cost and Composition of Major Production and Margin Items: Wheat Flour, China and Zambia

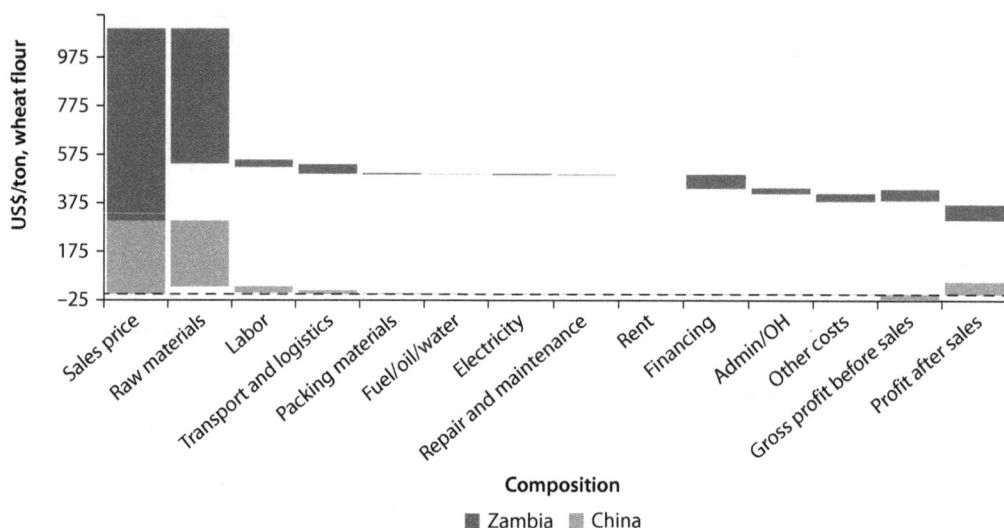

Composition

■ Zambia ▨ China

Source: GDS 2011.
Note: Admin/OH = administration/overhead.

drugs, and veterinary care—is high because of inadequate supply, high transport costs, and market imperfections.[9] Similarly, most fertilizer is imported, at high cost; farmers cite fertilizer costs as a key contributor to the high cost of producing wheat; fertilizer accounts for up to 40 percent of the variable costs of wheat production (Meas Consultancy and Training Services 2011). In addition to the high transport costs, several policy and administrative issues add to the high cost of imported fertilizer (Engman and others 2010).

– *Heavy reliance on rainfed agriculture:* Only 170,000 hectares of a potential of more than 500,000 hectares are under irrigation (MOF 2011).

– *Knowledge gaps:* This includes inadequate research and development in improved seed varieties and livestock practices. It also includes weak business orientation and poor farming and animal husbandry practices among farmers.

– *Limited access by farmers to finance and other infrastructure, including both hard infrastructure (such as transport and electric power) and soft infrastructure (such as education):* Access to finance is especially limited among small and medium farmers because the financial sector considers agriculture a high-risk activity.[10]

• *Inefficiencies in the processing segment of the value chain:* While Zambia's lack of competitiveness in wheat flour is explained largely by the high cost of wheat, high processing costs also contribute (related to the high costs of labor, packaging, and fuel and high overhead). Millers pass a large share of the price of already expensive wheat on to the price of flour because of their inability to obtain favorable prices for bran and other wheat by-products, in part because of regulatory constraints (see table 9.1). Similar inefficiencies in the dairy industry compound the impact of the high cost of raw milk. The industry is dominated by four or five large processors that control more than 90 percent of the market. Many processing plants suffer from low capacity utilization and, therefore, have relatively high fixed costs. The lack of domestic competition means that there is little pressure to increase efficiency and innovate. Larger plants are spread out across the country and do not compete head-to-head. The only competition comes from smaller plants that do not have sufficient market shares to influence the market (World Bank 2011a).

Recommendations

Improving the competitiveness of the agribusiness sector in Zambia would require that agricultural productivity be improved and that agricultural production costs be reduced given that agricultural inputs account for most of the cost of processed products. For example, the cost of wheat in Zambia is well above the cost of wheat in the other four countries in our study, and wheat milling is unlikely to become internationally competitive unless Zambian wheat prices are lowered. Thus, the recommended policy interventions focus primarily on the agricultural production end of the agribusiness supply chain:

- *Liberalize the input (agriculture) and output markets:*
  - In particular, the government needs to be more consistent and predictable in imposing bans on wheat exports and imports. This would reduce business uncertainty and encourage investment in and lending to agricultural businesses. A recent study has found that sudden government interventions in agricultural markets (including changes in import and export restrictions and duties), by weakening price signals and making accurate planning impossible, represent a major contribution to the risky lending environment for agriculture in Zambia that discourages lending (Taylor, Dougherty, and Munro 2009).
  - The government needs to assess the costs and benefits of other actions, such as removing the import duties on agricultural products, and to formulate an appropriate policy decision. For example, the Economics Association of Zambia has argued for the removal of the 15 percent import duty on wheat and the removal of all import and excise duties on imported inputs for wheat and flour production (tractors, spare tractor parts, tires, irrigation equipment, chemicals, and milling equipment). They argue that this could lower production costs sufficiently to enable wheat and milling companies to compete with imports and that the increased tax revenue from the greater demand for bread and wheat products could compensate the government for the lost income from duties (Hantuba 2009).

Similarly, the Zambia National Farmers Union has argued for a zero-rating of the value added tax on wheat, wheat flour, and simple agricultural equipment to enable domestic wheat to compete with subsidized, duty-exempt regional imports (ZNFU 2012).

- The sequencing of the liberalization of inputs and outputs is a key to policy success. In the past, the liberalization of the output market before the input market led to a collapse of the industry as imports flooded the domestic market before domestic industries had had a chance to adjust. It is therefore critical that inputs be liberalized first, although this will induce a temporary increase in the effective rate of protection, which will disappear once the output market is completely liberalized.

• *Promote foreign direct investment in input industries:* This would include facilitating access to agricultural land for investors interested in producing crops or livestock with high potential. A fully transparent and inclusive process is needed to ensure that local communities benefit and that environmental issues are addressed. The concept of farm blocks—large areas of agricultural land provided with services such as roads, dams, and electricity—has become popular in Zambia, and the SNDP calls for the establishment of three farm blocks by 2015. The 100,000-hectare Nansanga farm block currently under development will grow wheat (among other crops) and incorporate agroprocessing facilities. More may need to be done to encourage investors, however, because only 2 of the 10 companies shortlisted by the government have submitted bids (Simpelwe 2011). In addition to agricultural production, industries that provide inputs to agriculture (such as fertilizer and drugs) could benefit from foreign investment.

• *Improve the access of small and medium agricultural enterprises to finance:* Reducing government intervention in agricultural markets or making government intervention more predictable, while reducing agricultural input costs, could enhance access to finance by lessening the risks of lending to small and medium agricultural enterprises. Access to finance could also be improved by making it easier for banks to accept alternative forms of collateral (such as warehouse receipts, crops in the ground, or the "chief's titles" that are used to secure loans to farmers who do not have individual and formal titles to their land); increasing awareness among banks about the agricultural sector; and addressing weaknesses in the legal and regulatory framework. Passage of the proposed amendment to the Agricultural Credit Act would facilitate the use of other types of collateral (see Taylor, Dougherty, and Munro 2009).

• *Improve the access of micro, small, and medium agricultural enterprises to training, land, and other infrastructure to raise productivity:* Plug-and-play industrial parks could encourage the entry of leading agribusiness enterprises and help greater-potential small and medium firms gain access to utilities, land, finance, and skills. Leading enterprises could link up with small farmers and provide technical assistance to encourage farmers to use more advanced farming and animal husbandry techniques and to begin to treat farming as a commercial activity.

Notes

1. Data of UN Comtrade (United Nations Commodity Trade Statistics Database), Statistics Division, Department of Economic and Social Affairs, United Nations, New York, http://comtrade.un.org/db.

2. Data of UN Comtrade (United Nations Commodity Trade Statistics Database), Statistics Division, Department of Economic and Social Affairs, United Nations, New York, http://comtrade.un.org/db.

3. There are discrepancies across the data recorded by various sources.

4. Compiled by Global Development Solutions (GDS 2011) based on data of UN Comtrade (United Nations Commodity Trade Statistics Database), Statistics Division, Department of Economic and Social Affairs, United Nations, New York, http://comtrade.un.org/db.

5. This would be so in the beef and dairy industries, for example (World Bank 2011a).

6. This section is based mainly on a detailed analysis of wheat flour and dairy; see the comparative value chain analysis in World Bank (2011b).

7. All land belongs to the state, and the president is trustee. Land is usually acquired from the state on a leasehold basis for up to 99 years on condition that the land be developed. Foreign companies seeking to acquire land may lease publicly held land or land that has already been acquired from the state by private parties. Zambia also scores poorly on the strength of legal rights for investors leasing industrial land (World Bank 2010).

8. For example, Statutory Instrument 18 of 2009 bans imports of wheat grain and wheat flour. Temporary bans have been imposed on both imports and exports to improve food security and encourage local industry or to respond to demands from the Zambia National Farmers Union for import bans or the Millers Association of Zambia for export bans (see Kuwema 2010; ZNFU 2009). As a result of such market restrictions, concerns have arisen about alleged hoarding by farmers and uneven wheat distribution, illegal imports, and domestic oversupply (see "Govt Working on Equitable Wheat Distribution," *Times of Zambia*, Ndola, Zambia, April 22, 2011; also see ZNFU n.d.).

9. There are only three large importers of semen, veterinary drugs, and medicines in Zambia because of the small market. Two are not distributors, but retail outlets that are based in Lusaka and are unable to cover the whole country. Drugs and medicines are therefore imported from South Africa in small quantities, making them more expensive. The high costs are passed on in the price of the final product or in reduced productivity (because the high cost of inputs deters farmers from using them). For more detail, see World Bank (2011a).

10. Among Zambian agricultural firms, access to electricity, water, and lending services is associated with higher productivity of 52, 23, and 44 percent, respectively (Conway and Shah 2010).

References

Conway, Patrick, and Manju K. Shah. 2010. "Zambia Business Survey: Who's Productive in Zambia's Private Sector? Evidence from the Zambia Business Survey." Zambia Business Forum, Private Sector Development Reform Program (Ministry of Commerce, Trade, and Industry), FinMark Trust, and World Bank, Lusaka.

Engman, Michael, Yasuo Konishi, Smita Kuriakose, Glen Surabian, Ranga R. Krishnamani, Manju K. Shah, Siobhan Murray, and Ganesh Rasagam. 2010. *Enabling Private Sector Development in the Landlocked Regions of the North-South Corridor.* Africa Finance and Private Sector Department, World Bank, Washington, DC.

GDS (Global Development Solutions). 2011. *The Value Chain and Feasibility Analysis; Domestic Resource Cost Analysis.* Vol. 2 of *Light Manufacturing in Africa: Targeted Policies to Enhance Private Investment and Create Jobs.* Washington, DC: World Bank. http://go.worldbank.org/6G2A3TFI20.

Hantuba, Muna. 2009. "Business Unusual: The Policy Implications for Zambia of the Global Economic Crisis." Paper presented at Economics Association of Zambia's "Economic Crisis Workshop," Economics Association of Zambia, Lusaka, March.

Kuwema, Moses. 2010. "ZNFU Reveals Interference from Millers on Wheat Import Ban." *Post Online,* Post Newspapers, Lusaka. http://www.postzambia.com/post-read_article.php?articleId=11950.

Meas Consultancy and Training Services. 2011. *Wheat Value Chain Study.* Lusaka: Agricultural Consultative Forum.

MOAC and MOLF (Zambia, Ministry of Agriculture and Co-operatives and Ministry of Livestock and Fisheries). 2010. "A Brief Presentation on Zambia's Investment Opportunities in Agriculture." Paper presented at Taj Pamodzi Hotel, Lusaka, January 26.

MOF (Zambia, Ministry of Finance and National Planning). 2011. *Sixth National Development Plan 2011–2015: "Sustained Economic Growth and Poverty Reduction."* Lusaka: MOF.

Simpelwe, Ndinawe. 2011. "ZDA Receives Only 2 Bids for Nansanga Bloc." *Post Online,* Post Newspapers, Lusaka. http://www.postzambia.com/post-read_article.php?articleId=21506.

Taylor, Michael, Joseph Dougherty, and Robert Munro. 2009. "Zambia's Agricultural Finance Market: Challenges and Opportunities." United States Agency for International Development and Zambia National Farmers Union, Lusaka.

World Bank. 2010. *Investing across Borders 2010: Indicators of Foreign Direct Investment Regulation in 87 Economies.* Washington, DC: Investment Climate Advisory Services, World Bank.

———. 2011a. "Zambia: What Would It Take for Zambia's Beef and Dairy Industries to Achieve Their Potential?" Report 62377-ZM, Finance and Private Sector Development Unit, Africa Region, World Bank, Washington, DC.

———. 2011b. *Background Papers.* Vol. 3 of *Light Manufacturing in Africa: Targeted Policies to Enhance Private Investment and Create Jobs.* Washington, DC: World Bank. http://go.worldbank.org/LIX5E1FI90.

ZNFU (Zambia National Farmers Union). 2009. "Head of State Upholds Wheat Import Ban." Press Release, ZNFU, Lusaka, June 30.

———. 2012. "The 2012 National Budget Submissions." ZNFU, Lusaka. http://www.znfu .org.zm/index.php?option=com_content&view=article&id=401:the-2012-national- budget-submissions&catid=35:position-papers&Itemid=66.

———. No date. "State of Agriculture, Maize and Wheat Marketing in Particular." Press Release, ZNFU, Lusaka.

CHAPTER 10

Synthesis: Reform and Policy Recommendations

This chapter synthesizes our study findings across the five sectors we have examined and discusses the implementation of reforms and our policy recommendations. Many of the recommendations in this report have been influenced by the experiences—both successes and failures—of developing countries that are farther along the development path, in addition to close analysis of the situation in Zambia.

Synthesis of the Results across the Five Sectors

This section summarizes the potential and the constraints in Zambia's light manufacturing sectors.

Zambia's Potential in Light Manufacturing

Several factors indicate that the potential for expanding Zambia's light manufacturing industries is good, as follows:

- The abundance of resources for use as key inputs with potential for competitive supply (for example, cotton, hides and skins, wood, metals, wheat and milk)
- Low wages in some sectors (relative to China), combined with high worker productivity in good practice firms in some sectors
- A growing domestic market and proximity to regional markets such as the Democratic Republic of Congo
- Duty-free access to the European Union, the United States, and regional markets in several light manufacturing products.

In the near term, the potential in all five sectors will likely be on replacing imports in the domestic market, though, in some sectors, there will be opportunities for regional exports. International exports may be possible over time in some sectors if production costs fall and productivity improves.

The Main Constraints on Competitiveness

The most important constraints on Zambia's competitiveness in light manufacturing originate in the input industries, particularly agriculture. These constraints are exacerbated by poor trade logistics, which increase the cost of imported alternatives. The situation is particularly bad for Zambian small and medium enterprises, the productivity of which suffers as a result of difficulties in accessing land, finance, skills, and other hard and soft infrastructure.

Constraints vary by sector and firm size. Table 10.1 shows the most important constraints on each of the sectors and distinguishes between smaller and larger firms.

Some of the policy recommendations in this report are consistent with the traditional investment climate agenda and seek to promote competition and reduce transaction costs (for example, improve trade logistics and lower import tariffs). However, the detailed sector-level diagnostics and cross-country comparisons conducted for this study allow more specific policy recommendations to be derived for each light manufacturing sector. Also, many of the key recommendations are related to input industries in light manufacturing and, as such, have often been overlooked.

Several findings emerge from the analysis in chapter 5–9, as follows:

- Examining the critical constraints individually by sector is important because the constraints and the needed policy measures to address the constraints differ by sector and by firm size.
- Tackling the agriculture reform agenda is fundamental to developing light manufacturing in Zambia. Reforms in the agriculture sector—where Zambia

Table 10.1 Constraints by Sector, Importance, and Firm Size, Zambia

Sector and firm size	Input industries	Land	Finance	Entrepreneurial skills	Worker skills	Trade logistics
Apparel						
Smaller	Important	Critical	Critical	Important	Important	
Larger	Important			Important		Critical
Leather products						
Smaller	Critical	Critical	Critical	Important		
Larger	Critical			Important		Critical
Wood products						
Smaller	Critical	Important	Important	Important	Important	
Larger	Critical	Important	Important	Important	Important	
Metal products						
Smaller	Critical	Important	Important	Important	Important	
Larger	Critical	Important	Important	Important	Important	
Agribusiness						
Smaller	Critical	Critical	Critical	Important	Important	
Larger	Critical	Critical	Important			

Source: World Bank compilation based on the analysis presented in chapters 5–9.
Note: Blank cells indicate that the issue is not a priority.

has untapped potential—will be critical to improving the competitiveness of three of the five light manufacturing sectors under examination (agribusiness, leather products, and wood products). The specific agricultural reform agenda deserves its own in-depth study and discussion, but the necessary reforms fall into two broad categories: liberalizing agricultural output and input markets in the proper order and facilitating access to rural land among good practice investors.

- Lowering import tariffs and improving trade logistics are crucial for facilitating the importation of key inputs that cannot be competitively produced in Zambia. Industries producing the necessary inputs should also be fostered by opening them to foreign direct investment and providing incentives to domestic producers to drive down the high prices. For goods such as cotton, leather, and wood, Zambia has an abundance of resources that can be sourced domestically if these products are targeted.
- Developing plug-and-play industrial parks and collateral markets will be important in all sectors.
- Encouraging foreign direct investment is vital in sectors with the most potential for exports. Critical reforms will need to be implemented first to make Zambia an attractive destination for foreign investment, and rent-seeking will need to be minimized.

Determining Priority Sectors

The choice of priority sectors should be based on sectoral comparative advantage. Chapter 1 discusses various methods to determine whether a country has a comparative advantage in a product or a sector. One method is to calculate the domestic resource cost (DRC) ratios discussed in chapter 1 (see also Bhagwati and Srinivasan 1980; Bruno 1972; Pack 1974, 1987). A ratio of less than 1 indicates that the cost of the domestic resources used to produce a unit of the product is less than the potential foreign exchange earnings from exporting the product. That means that the country has a comparative advantage in the product and that therefore the government has a rationale for fostering exports in the product. A ratio of greater than 1 indicates that the cost of the domestic resources spent to produce the good for the domestic market is more than the foreign exchange spent to import the good and that the country does not have a comparative advantage in the good. If the government is supporting import-substituting policies for this good, it should discontinue them.

The DRC ratios are calculated on an ex post basis according to the existing resource endowment and policies. Policy reforms could change the DRC value over time. For industries that pass the DRC test, whether in exports or in import substitution, following through by conducting integrated value chain studies can help map constraints into policy recommendations and identify exactly what will be required of the government in promoting the expansion of the identified industry.

Table 10.2 shows the DRC ratios for each product for which we have carried out a comparative value chain analysis. Based on these and other criteria, the

Table 10.2 Domestic Resource Cost Ratios for Selected Products, Zambia

Leather loafers	Boxer briefs	Wooden chairs	Wheat milling	Crown corks
Above 1.0, based on the ERR	Above 1.0 (based on ERR), but could be competitive with reasonable productivity improvements	1.20–2.47	0.75–1.33	0.68

Source: GDS 2011.

Note: The DRC domestic resource cost (DRC) is defined as $d_j = \dfrac{-\sum_{s=2}^{m} \overline{f_{sj}} v_s}{u_j - m_j}$, where d_j is the DRC of product j, m is the number of primary factors and n number of products; v_s is the accounting (shadow) price for the sth primary factor ($s = 1$ is the foreign exchange), f_{sj} is the difference between the marginal dollar revenue of commodity j (u_j) and the (marginal) dollar import requirements for the unit production of commodity j (m_j); and a *bar* represents the total (direct and indirect) primary factors of production. ERR = economic rate of return.

sectoral priority in decreasing order is agribusiness, metal products, leather products, apparel, and wood products. However, for the special case of crown corks and metal products, see chapter 8.

Another practical way that we recommend to identify the existing products or sectors a country should be producing or producing in is to follow those in which private sector initiatives (without any government interventions) have been successful. In effect, this is how local governments in China assist enterprises to grow: they wait until private enterprises have become successful and then assist them to expand (Dinh and others 2013).

Institutional Arrangements for Implementation

If the proposed agenda is to be successful in attracting domestic and foreign investors to light manufacturing in Zambia, there needs to be a credible commitment to the policy agenda from the highest level of government and, thereby, assurance that the investments would be safe from government interference. Given the strategic importance and feasibility of such an opportunity, it is important that the Zambian government put in place a dedicated high-level implementation task team, together with transparent, inclusive, and professional processes, to develop and implement a reform program that will encourage the growth of high-potential light manufacturing sectors. Such a task team would need to be technically knowledgeable and adequately resourced and have the appropriate authority to take necessary action.

This model has been followed by most successful developing economies (such as Botswana, Cape Verde, Malaysia, Mauritius, and Taiwan, China) at the outset of their economic transformation journey (Criscuolo and Palmade 2008). The combination of skills, access, and resources gave the reform teams in these economies the influence needed to steer an ambitious (yet focused) policy agenda despite opposing interests. Such teams have typically been charged with designing or updating the reform strategy, engaging and negotiating with potential leading investors, mobilizing the support of development partners, supporting and monitoring the implementation of key government initiatives, and keeping government leaders informed and committed.

Political Economy

The policy approach outlined in this chapter proposes that proactive government support should be provided to the light manufacturing sector through technical assistance, input industry development, and the establishment of plug-and-play industrial parks, among other measures. The aims of these policies are to increase competition and raise the capacity of all firms to compete, thereby leveling the playing field across types of firms. As with any active government policy, there is a risk of creating rents or policy-induced profits. Policy and implementation should work to ensure that the beneficiaries of government policy are determined by market forces and not by the special interests of government officials or as a result of rent-seeking behavior.

There are several reasons why the proposed policy measures could minimize rent-seeking opportunities in implementation, as follows:

• The proposed approach and the sector-specific support are focused on sectors consistent with Zambia's latent comparative advantage. Thus, the magnitude of government intervention is likely to be small and can be rapidly scaled back as new information is gathered.
• The extent and costs of rent-seeking can be minimized through clear, inclusive, and transparent government policies for which government officials can be held accountable. The private sector could thus reliably be included in the investment decision. Policies should be focused on providing public goods that benefit all firms equally, and, if more direct support is offered, there should be a competitive process through which firms could access the support. For example, access to a new industrial park must be fair and open and allow no opportunity for rent-seeking behavior. The government must be clear on the objectives of the industrial park.
• The reform should begin with pilot case studies and be continually revised and updated. In addition, implementation should be decentralized to increase participation by the private sector, strengthen accountability, and foster competition among local governments.
• The government must be ready to withdraw support promptly from industries that prove inefficient or nonviable.
• One of the best ways for the government to facilitate robust private sector growth is by maintaining a stable and conducive macroeconomic environment and ensuring that natural resources are well managed. Such facilitation policies are also endogenous to the growth process if the selection of industries is consistent with the country's comparative advantages.

The Fiscal Cost and Feasibility of the Policy Recommendations

Overall, the proposed reform program for Zambia is attainable because the recommendations are specific and few in number and can be packaged and prioritized (with the help of development partners) along the most promising sectors. The cost and the technical and political economy feasibility of each of the proposed recommendations are discussed below. Although the proposed policies are designed to eliminate rent-seeking, some parts of the government may still find ways to favor connected firms and extract rents from others. For this reason, it will be essential to secure and sustain the commitment of the top level of government to the growth and jobs agenda and to put in place transparent and professional processes that provide controls and incentives for proper implementation.

Table 10.3 shows the estimated fiscal cost and the political economy feasibility of each of the proposed measures. Successful implementation of these actions will rely on the leadership provided by a high-level task team.

Policy Implementation Issues

There are several key requirements for effective implementation of the proposed policy actions, including garnering high-level political commitment, ensuring effective policy coordination, building strong public-private partnerships, coordinating donor assistance, and addressing the governance and political economy issues.

Garnering High-Level Political Commitment
The proposed policy actions contemplate new investments by local and foreign investors to expand production and introduce new technology in the selected sectors. Prospective investors would require assurances from the highest level of the government that the program and supportive policy agenda would continue. Setting up a high-level committee in the Zambia Business Forum with direct access to top government leaders to oversee implementation of the program would give the necessary credibility to the program.[1]

Ensuring Effective Policy Coordination
Responsibility for formulating and implementing the proposed reforms would lie with a variety of public and private institutions, each focusing on an aspect of the program. Effective coordination to synchronize policy actions would be essential to success. Currently, the agency responsible for implementing Zambia's industrial strategy is the Zambia Development Agency (ZDA). The consolidation of various development institutions under the ZDA is a positive initial step toward more effective policy coordination. Strengthening the sectoral units under the Secretariat of Sectoral Policies would be one way for the ZDA to institutionalize policy coordination. Regular meetings with relevant agencies under the ZDA sectoral secretariats would strengthen coordination.

Building Strong Public-Private Partnerships
The capacity to formulate and implement policies is weak in both the public and private sectors. Building a strong partnership in policy formulation and implementation is therefore necessary to enhance the limited capacity and achieve effective results. This will also help reduce the long-standing suspicion between these two sectors. Implementation capacity is weakest at the district level, where

Table 10.3 Fiscal Cost and Political Economy Feasibility: Reform Policy Measures, Zambia

Measure	Fiscal cost	Political economy feasibility
Liberalize agriculture output and input markets	Many actions are primarily administrative (for example, removing export bans and reforming agricultural marketing practices).	Such reforms can be politically and socially sensitive. For example, fully liberalizing the leather trade would benefit cattle ranchers, but would go against the short-term interests of tanneries; food export bans (on wheat, for example) would need to be considered in the context of food security. Based on its manifesto, the government seems interested in reducing the policy uncertainty—such as on import and export bans—affecting key crops (Patriotic Front 2011). However, the type of policies to be introduced is still unclear. The government is likely to face pressure from different sides (for example, millers, who favor export bans, and farmers, who favor import bans).[a]
Eliminate import tariffs on the main inputs for all firms, even nonexporters	Total import duties from the five sectors amounted to K 210 billion in 2010 (1.7 percent of total tax revenue). Hence, removing import duties on the inputs of the light manufacturing sector would not cost more than 1.7 percent of total tax revenue and can be easily made up by excise taxes if needed.	Import tariffs afford protection to domestic suppliers, and, so, there is potential for these suppliers to lose out in the short run if tariffs are eliminated. The case therefore needs to be made that all will benefit in the long run, and, if necessary, parallel interventions to support productivity improvements in domestic production should balance out the loss to local farmers.
Facilitate access to land by strategic investors in the agriculture, livestock, and forestry sectors	This recommendation should generate (local) government revenues because the private sector should be asked to pay to lease land. The financing cost of connecting the land to the road network and utilities could be absorbed by the private investor in exchange for a reduction in the land lease. Carbon credit financing should be available for wood plantations on degraded land.	This is an extremely politically, socially, and environmentally sensitive topic that will require the government to rely on a fully transparent, inclusive, and highly professional process. (Principles for responsible agricultural investments are being developed by the international community.)
Facilitate entry (without rents) of leading investors along the value chains (may include public-private partnerships)	Development partners could provide financial and technical support to a good practice investment promotion agency and for a good policy. The cost of any investment incentives and any government contribution to public-private partnerships would need to be considered.	Zambia is open to foreign investment.[b] Any donor support programs would need to be designed carefully to take into account the lessons of experience in supporting Zambia's investment promotion agency, the Zambia Development Agency (ZDA). Despite recent reforms and donor support, ZDA's performance is still rated weak on both a regional and international basis (World Bank 2009). The investment promotion agency would need to follow strict and transparent procedures to minimize the risk of capture by well-connected firms. The strategy should be to design interventions that are replicable or benefit all firms in the sector and create a level playing field. Establishing public-private partnerships for light manufacturing is in line with the new government's policy to "rejuvenate the manufacturing sector through the promotion of public–private partnership investment, in order to enhance the establishment of competitive manufacturing industries whose products will find markets outside Zambia."[c]

table continues next page

101

Table 10.3 Fiscal Cost and Political Economy Feasibility: Reform Policy Measures, Zambia *(continued)*

Measure	Fiscal cost	Political economy feasibility
Establish industrial parks	Because tenants would cover the operating and maintenance costs of these parks, the cost to the government would be limited to the financing cost of developing the parks. The Sixth National Development Plan (SNDP) envisages a total government contribution of K 45 billion ($9.4 million) toward establishing four multifacility economic zones in 2011–15. As in China and Vietnam, private developers (including foreign developers) and banks could help finance such zones.	The government seems interested in establishing industrial parks, and some efforts are already under way. The SNDP intends that four new multifacility economic zones and two industrial zones will be operational by 2015, and the new government's manifesto mentions establishing special economic zones, industrial parks, logistics parks, industrial estates, and innovation hubs (Patriotic Front 2011). Multifacility economic zones located next to key border crossing points are also envisaged. The design of such zones should be influenced by both successful and unsuccessful experiences. The objectives, characteristics, and operational procedures of such zones must be appropriate, transparent, and indigenous, and small companies should have a fair opportunity to participate in the zones.[d] The locations must be based on clear economic considerations (for example, close to key domestic markets or international borders).
Support the development of small and medium enterprise clusters and business incubators	Cluster development and business incubators could be supported by development partners or be established as part of wider industrial park initiatives.	No major political economy challenge is expected.
Support the development of partnerships across segments of the value chains	Large companies in the value chains may also be willing to support partnerships with farmers, small and medium enterprises, and others (as in the Dunavant and Zambeef initiatives).	Such policies can be win-win; a number of partnership initiatives have the potential to benefit large companies, small and medium enterprises, and farmers.
Support improvements in managerial and technical skills, particularly among small and medium enterprises	The cost of providing management and technical training is high initially because expatriate trainers are required. It falls significantly once local trainers have been trained. Experienced world-class providers should be leveraged, together with state-of-the-art methods of evaluation (for example, randomized evaluation). Kaizen training may be a low-cost means of supporting the development of management skills.	No major political economy challenge is expected.

table continues next page

Table 10.3 Fiscal Cost and Political Economy Feasibility: Reform Policy Measures, Zambia *(continued)*

Measure	Fiscal cost	Political economy feasibility
Establish one-stop border posts	For example, in the construction of the Chirundu one-stop border post, the government contributed approximately US$30 million for infrastructure, and donors and the government of Zimbabwe also contributed.[e] The government has been seeking investors for a one-stop post at the border with the Democratic Republic of Congo, at an estimated cost of $16 million (ZDA and CBC 2011). According to the SNDP, a public–private partnership approach (a build-operate-transfer arrangement) will be used to improve infrastructure at a number of border posts (MOF 2011). In the longer term, a more efficient border with more trade and less potential for corruption could increase government revenues.	Requires high-level government support and strong collaboration among countries and agencies. Experience suggests that, although this may be challenging, it is possible. (The Chirundu one-stop border post has reportedly benefited from strong commitment from both governments, as well as support from the private sector.) The establishment of such posts is already an objective of the SNDP, which has a target of three one-stop border posts by 2015.
Reduce the time spent preparing letters of credit	The support of development partners could be harnessed to expand and improve the credit reference system.	
Develop an improved, multimodal transportation system	Private sector investment in transport infrastructure could reduce some of the costs to the government. Based on the SNDP, a public–private partnership approach is envisaged for a number of transport projects (MOF 2011). Appropriately structured road user charges and fuel taxes could reduce government costs for road maintenance.	In selecting transportation projects, the government may face some conflict between economic feasibility and social and political considerations. Given Zambia's landlocked status, it will be important to coordinate with neighboring countries.
Facilitate the use of new types of collateral (of particular benefit to small and medium enterprises)	The cost would be mostly in the form of technical assistance to improve the regulatory framework and collateral registries. This could be financed with the support of development partners.	There may be some social and political challenges associated with introducing land titles to facilitate the use of land as collateral.

table continues next page

Table 10.3 Fiscal Cost and Political Economy Feasibility: Reform Policy Measures, Zambia *(continued)*

Measure	Fiscal cost	Political economy feasibility
Reform the labor market (of particular benefit to the apparel sector)	The financial cost in implementing reforms (mainly administrative measures) is low. There may be potential for increased government revenue from payroll taxes.	Even though existing labor laws and regulations benefit only a tiny proportion of the workforce (at the expense of all others), such labor reforms are always politically sensitive. Based on its manifesto, the new government may plan to undertake a review of labor legislation (Patriotic Front 2011). Trade unions may resist change.[f]
Locally source a larger share of government purchases of light manufacturing products	The fiscal cost to the government is not clear. Locally made goods may be more expensive than imported goods, but eliminating the middlemen could reduce the cost of purchases to the government.	Such action is consistent with World Trade Organization rules. Existing suppliers (local middlemen) are likely to resist such action. The policy would need to be implemented carefully and in a fully transparent manner to ensure that it is efficient and achieves the desired objectives, as well as to ensure adequate quality in the products the government procures. The World Bank Country Procurement Assessment Reports can help ensure transparency in this context.[g] The capacity of an individual local company may not be sufficient to meet government demand, but this could be addressed by dividing purchases into smaller parts, organizing the supply of goods cooperatively and led by a larger company, and so on.
Expand the livestock industry (of benefit to the leather and agribusiness sectors)	There is a range of possible actions, each with associated costs. For example, a study of the U.S. Agency for International Development (USAID 2008) estimated that Ethiopia could reduce the incidence of ectoparasites from 90 to only 5 percent with four treatments a year for each animal, costing about $0.10 each. The livestock industry has tended to be at a disadvantage in terms of government funding; the vast majority of agricultural funding allocation has typically gone to crops (mostly the fertilizer support program).	Some actions are likely to be easier than others to implement. For example, establishing a disease-free zone is likely to be complex (in sociopolitical and technical terms). The approach to disease control would need to be regional. Livestock has been receiving more government attention in recent years. (A dedicated livestock ministry was established in 2009, although it was recently remerged with agriculture, and the budget allocation was increased.) The new government's policy is still not clear, but, based on the government's manifesto, livestock restocking and breeding and combating disease appear to be priorities (Patriotic Front 2011).
Curtail the illegal trade in wood (of benefit to wood products)	The government could ultimately benefit financially if illegal logging and exports are curtailed.[h]	This is unlikely to be easy, and it is not clear that existing institutions have the capacity or staff to achieve this. Furthermore, there may be competing or vested interests at play.

table continues next page

Table 10.3 Fiscal Cost and Political Economy Feasibility: Reform Policy Measures, Zambia *(continued)*

Measure	Fiscal cost	Political economy feasibility
Encourage the exploration and exploitation of iron ore deposits (of benefit to the metal products sector)	Some investment incentives may need to be provided to encourage the private sector. If an appropriate taxation system is in place, this step should, in time, have a significant positive impact on government revenue.	A government interest seems to be in place. The manifesto expresses interest in promoting investment in the exploitation of minerals other than copper (Patriotic Front 2011). However, mining can be a highly politically and socially sensitive issue. The government should leverage its own experience in copper mining and the extensive worldwide experience in overcoming the technical, social, environmental, and political economy challenges that would be involved.

Source: World Bank compilation.

a. For an example of the sensitivities involved, see Sinyangwe (2011).

b. See World Bank (2010). All 33 sectors covered by the indicators, including light manufacturing, are fully open to foreign equity ownership.

c. See page 17, "Zambia: President Sata's Inaugural Speech to the Eleventh National Assembly," Press Release, *Times of Zambia*, Ndola, Zambia, October 15, 2011, http://allafrica.com/stories/201110171433.html.

d. There has been some recent controversy and confusion over government policy on multifacility economic zones and the extent to which smaller, indigenous firms could benefit from them.

e. "Banda, Mugabe to Launch One-Stop Border," *Times of Zambia*, Ndola, Zambia, December 2, 2009.

f. Available information from the 2009 Investment Climate Assessment indicates that about 20 percent of the workers in the manufacturing sector (medium and large firms) are unionized and that large firms are much more likely to have unionized workers (World Bank 2009). A separate survey reveals that only 5 percent of the workers in small and medium manufacturing enterprises in Zambia are unionized (see World Bank 2011).

g. See "Assessment of Country's Public Procurement System," World Bank, Washington, DC, http://go.worldbank.org/RZ7CHIRF60.

h. For example, the Timber Producers Association of Zambia estimates that Zambia lost around K 80 billion ($17 million) in 2007 in uncollected timber revenues following the government's decision to ban timber exports to member countries of the Southern African Development Community, which resulted in smuggling. See "Zambia Loses Money on Timber Following Ban on Exports," illegal-logging.info, London, June 19, 2008, http://www.illegal-logging.info/item_single.php?it_id=2740&it=news.

strong efforts are needed to assist light manufacturing enterprises, particularly micro and small enterprises. Effective partnerships among local governments, the local offices of the ZDA, sectoral associations, and other public and private institutions would bridge capacity gaps and improve the harmonization and coordination of policies. Public-private partnerships are possible in other areas, including micro and small enterprise financing, entrepreneurship, and technical training. Zambian light manufacturing could be revived if the government and the private sector collaborate effectively.

Coordinating Donor Assistance

Substantial donor assistance will be needed to implement the proposed program, particularly in areas such as building capacity in public and private institutions, assisting agencies that support small and medium enterprises, setting up vocational training and business incubation facilities, and strengthening business associations. Scores of donor programs already exist in these and other areas. The major bilateral donor organizations include the European Commission, the Japan International Cooperation Agency, the Nordic country aid agencies, the U.K. Department for International Development, the United Nations Conference on Trade and Development, the United Nations Industrial Development Organization, and the U.S. Agency for International Development. The impact of these programs has been limited because of the small size of some and the lack of local capacity to sustain the programs after donor support ends. Coordination of the donor programs under the leadership of the government is necessary to avoid overlaps, combine smaller programs for larger impact, and ensure that the programs are demand-driven and cover components of the light manufacturing program.

Addressing the Governance and Political Economy Issues

The suggested policy package includes market-based policies, as well as selective government interventions. Three principles must be followed to avoid serious governance shortcomings. First, government interventions should not aim to protect some favored companies. They should focus on improving the policy environment for all companies in the selected sectors with latent comparative advantage and allow unsuccessful companies to fail. Second, if subsidies and other supportive policies are warranted, they should target the sectors with latent comparative advantage to encourage new entrants, and they should remain in place only for a short time. Third, a key objective of the interventions should be to foster competition, for example, by reducing the entry costs and the risks.

Note

1. The Zambia Business Forum is an apex business body that interacts with the government and donors on economic issues. Its membership includes nine major business associations, including the Zambia Association of Manufacturers, the Zambia Chamber of Small and Medium Business Associations, and the Zambia Association of Chambers of Commerce and Industry. The forum is financed through membership fees and grants from the donor community.

References

Bhagwati, Jagdish N., and T. N. Srinivasan. 1980. "Domestic Resource Costs, Effective Rates of Protection, and Project Analysis in Tariff-Distorted Economies." *Quarterly Journal of Economics* 94 (1): 205–09.

Bruno, Michael B. 1972. "Domestic Resource Costs and Effective Protection: Clarifications and Synthesis." *Journal of Political Economy* 80 (1): 16–33.

Criscuolo, Alberto, and Vincent Palmade. 2008. "Reform Teams: How the Most Successful Reformers Organized Themselves." Public Policy for the Private Sector Note 318, World Bank, Washington, DC. http://rru.worldbank.org/documents/publicpolicy-journal/318Ciscuolo_Palmade.pdf.

Dinh, Hinh T., Thomas G. Rawski, Ali Zafar, and Lihong Wang. 2013. *Tales from the Development Frontier: How China and Other Countries Harness Light Manufacturing to Create Jobs and Prosperity.* With contributions by Eleonora Mavroeidi, Xin Tong, and Pengfei Li. Washington, DC: World Bank.

GDS (Global Development Solutions). 2011. *The Value Chain and Feasibility Analysis; Domestic Resource Cost Analysis.* Vol. 2 of *Light Manufacturing in Africa: Targeted Policies to Enhance Private Investment and Create Jobs.* Washington, DC: World Bank. http://go.worldbank.org/6G2A3TFI20.

MOF (Zambia, Ministry of Finance and National Planning). 2011. *Sixth National Development Plan 2011–2015: "Sustained Economic Growth and Poverty Reduction."* Lusaka: MOF.

Pack, Howard. 1974. "The Employment-Output Trade-Off in LDC's: A Microeconomic Approach." *Oxford Economic Papers* 26 (3): 388–404.

———. 1987. *Productivity, Technology, and Industrial Development: A Case Study in Textiles.* Washington, DC: World Bank; New York: Oxford University Press.

Patriotic Front. 2011. "Patriotic Front 2011–2016 Manifesto." Office of the Secretary General, Patriotic Front, Lusaka.

Sinyangwe, Chiwoyu. 2011. "ZNFU Calls for Cottan's Arrest." *The Post Online*, January 10. http://www.postzambia.com/post-read_article.php?articleId=17122.

World Bank. 2009. "Global Investment Promotion Benchmarking Report: Eyes on COMESA." Investment Climate Advisory Services, Washington, DC.

———. 2010. *Investing across Borders 2010: Indicators of Foreign Direct Investment Regulation in 87 Economies.* Washington, DC: Investment Climate Advisory Services, World Bank.

———. 2011. *Background Papers.* Vol. 3 of *Light Manufacturing in Africa: Targeted Policies to Enhance Private Investment and Create Jobs.* Washington, DC: World Bank. http://go.worldbank.org/LIX5E1FI90.

USAID (U.S. Agency for International Development). 2008. "Success Story: Ethiopians Learning to Fight Ectoparasites." Financial Transactions and Reports Analysis, USAID, Washington, DC.

ZDA (Zambia Development Agency) and CBC (Commonwealth Business Council). 2011. "Investment Project Profiles." Zambia Investment Forum, Lusaka.

green
press
INITIATIVE

www.ingramcontent.com/pod-product-compliance
Lightning Source LLC
Chambersburg PA
CBHW080617270326
41928CB00016B/3105